Sunset

PATIO ROOFS &
gazebos

EDITED BY DON VANDERVORT AND THE EDITORS OF SUNSET BOOKS

SUNSET BOOKS • MENLO PARK, CALIFORNIA

SUNSET BOOKS

Vice President & General Manager: Richard A. Smeby
Vice President & Editorial Director: Bob Doyle
Production Director: Lory Day
Art Director: Vasken Guiragossian
Director of Operations: Rosann Sutherland
Senior Editor: Marianne Lipanovich

**Patio Roofs & Gazebos was produced
in conjunction with HomeTips**

Editor: Don Vandervort
Managing Editor: Louise Damberg
Illustrator: Bill Oetinger
Graphic Designer: Dan Nadeau
Contributing Editors: Joe Truini,
    Roy Barnhart, Peter O. Whiteley
Production Coordinator: Danielle Javier
Proofreader: Lisa Black
Editorial Assistant: Kit Vandervort

Cover: Design by Vasken Guiragossian.
Photography by Philip Harvey. Photo styling by JoAnn
Masaoka Van Atta. Landscape Architect: L. Ransohoff,
Blanchfield, Jones, Inc. Gazebo by Dalton Pavilions Inc.

For additional copies of *Patio Roofs & Gazebos*
or any other Sunset book, call 1-800-526-5111
or visit us at www.sunsetbooks.com.

CONTENTS

a new patio roof, overhead, or gazebo can dramatically increase your enjoyment of your home's outdoor areas while serving as a major architectural and landscaping element. It can invite guests and family outdoors, effectively expanding your home's living areas and providing a place for quiet conversation, relaxation, or entertaining. And while it enhances the enjoyment and visual interest of outdoor areas, it can often increase a home's value, too.

The way a structure serves depends upon how it's built. A solid patio roof will shelter a deck or patio from harsh weather. Shade structures with open-style roofing can cool a patio—or interior rooms on the sunny side of a house—yet still admit light. A garden structure such as a gazebo can offer a focal point to draw guests into the garden.

To design a structure that meets your family's needs effectively and efficiently, first think about how you want the structure to function and prioritize the tasks you'd like it to perform. Analyze various sites around your house, keeping your garden's microclimate in mind; study up on materials choices; and get your design ideas on paper.

Whether you want to conceptualize and build a structure yourself or you plan to hire a professional, this chapter will help you understand the entire planning and design process.

planning and

design

THE PLANNING PROCESS

When you embark on a home-improvement project, the natural tendency is to want to jump right in and start building. Resist the temptation! With any building project, planning is the most important step. Without planning, it's too easy to make mistakes that are time-consuming at best and costly at worst.

Planning is all the more important when you're building a structure that will be a major addition to your house or landscape, and is capable of resisting the elements as well as functioning in certain ways. In addition to developing a design that fulfills your needs and blends with your home's design, you must consider site, climate, legal restrictions, cost, and myriad other factors.

EVALUATING YOUR NEEDS

If you can successfully replicate in your yard one of the shelters from this book, great! But it's more likely that the soil conditions of your property, the structure's proposed site, or even local building code requirements are different from those that governed any particular project here. Consider, then, how you might adapt a project to work for you. Unless you're experienced in design and construction techniques, it's usually best to consult with a professional for expert advice on building specifications. For information on working with professionals, see page 10.

Think about whether you want your structure to:

CONTROL SUN EXPOSURE An overhead on an exposed patio or deck can convert a sun-baked surface into a cool, inviting oasis. By casting shade across the house, it can also reduce the sun's glare and lower air-conditioning bills during the warm summer months.

SHED RAIN In a wet climate, a solid roof shelters a deck or patio from rain, extending the period the outdoor area

TOP: A garden shelter, when coupled with screening, can provide a measure of privacy and a feeling of comfort and enclosure.

ABOVE: This shade structure performs double duty, cooling the patio area below and reducing heat build-up and the sun's glare on the house's wall of windows.

LEFT: Lush climbing vines, supported by sturdy lattice panels, control sun exposure to this patio while at the same time turning the dining area into a verdant outdoor room.

can be used. In addition, a solid, well-designed patio roof can shelter doorways or help direct rainwater away from the house. As a bonus, outdoor furniture and equipment can be safely stored beneath it.

EXTEND LIVABLE SPACE Patios, poolside pavilions, and garden entertainment structures can draw guests into the yard, taking the burden off your home's kitchen and dining and living

areas. When outdoor centers are equipped with barbecues, work surfaces, and seating areas, they make entertaining a delight.

ADD VISUAL INTEREST A well-designed patio roof or deck overhead can dramatically improve your home's appearance, giving a nondescript roof line a new dimension. At poolside or in the garden, a pavilion or gazebo introduces a dynamic architectural element and a focal point for your landscaping. A series of overheads can integrate several backyard features, such as a deck, a pool, and a dining area.

INCREASE A HOME'S VALUE A new patio roof or gazebo, if well designed and built with care, will enhance your home's livability and appearance, adding to its resale value.

ENHANCE PRIVACY & COMFORT If your home is located in an area where houses are built close together, an outdoor shelter provides a measure of pri-

Because a gazebo is a focal point of a yard's landscaping, its siting must be carefully considered.

A well-designed patio roof harmonizes with the architectural style of the house; here, vegas — rustic lodge poles — are the perfect complement to a Southwestern-style home.

vacy and a feeling of enclosure. Regardless of the size of your yard, the structure can welcome you outdoors.

DESIGN BASICS

An outdoor structure should not block desired light or views, and it should harmonize with the architectural style of your home. Though it's not essential that an overhead be built from the same materials as the house, the new structure should blend harmoniously with them.

Consider sight lines. When you're standing inside looking out, beams that are too low will pull your viewable horizon down. Plan the overhead's height so it doesn't block a nice view. Generally, the lowest beam should not be placed less than 6 feet, 8 inches from the finished floor surface.

CHOOSING A SITE

For many overhead projects, the site is predetermined by your needs. Your deck requires shelter from the ele-

ments. The spa would benefit from an overhead. The pool area would be enhanced by an entertainment center.

If, on the other hand, you're rethinking your yard, or developing a comprehensive landscaping plan, you'll want to review a few basic site considerations. (For information on legal restrictions, see page 8.)

RELATIONSHIP TO THE HOUSE As you consider different locations for an overhead or gazebo, evaluate each site in terms of its accessibility to and from the house, any established traffic patterns, and any views you want to preserve or obscure.

RELATIONSHIP TO THE YARD Study your yard—its contours, views, the location of trees, and any other relevant elements—and try to maximize its assets. At the same time, be aware of drop-offs, areas that drain poorly or have unstable soil, and exposures to blazing sun or strong winds.

MICROCLIMATES

Sun, wind, and rain affect different parts of your property in different ways.

If you're planning to build an overhead, you'll need to understand your yard's microclimate.

THE SUN'S PATH In general, a patio that faces north is cool because the sun rarely shines on it. A south-facing patio is usually warm because, from sunrise to sunset, the sun never leaves it. Patios on the east side stay cool because they receive only morning sun, while west-facing areas can be uncomfortably hot because they absorb the full force of the sun's mid-afternoon rays. Of course, you'll need to adjust these rules to suit your climate.

The sun crosses the sky in an arc that changes slightly every day, becoming lower in winter and higher in summer (see the illustration below). In the dead of winter, it tracks across the sky at a low angle, throwing long shadows; on long summer days, it moves overhead at a very high angle. The farther north you live from the equator, the more extreme are the angles.

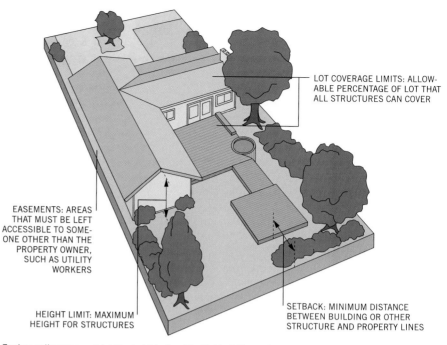

LOT COVERAGE LIMITS: ALLOWABLE PERCENTAGE OF LOT THAT ALL STRUCTURES CAN COVER

EASEMENTS: AREAS THAT MUST BE LEFT ACCESSIBLE TO SOMEONE OTHER THAN THE PROPERTY OWNER, SUCH AS UTILITY WORKERS

HEIGHT LIMIT: MAXIMUM HEIGHT FOR STRUCTURES

SETBACK: MINIMUM DISTANCE BETWEEN BUILDING OR OTHER STRUCTURE AND PROPERTY LINES

Zoning ordinances restrict the height of residential buildings, limit lot coverage, specify setbacks and easements, and, in some cases, set design standards.

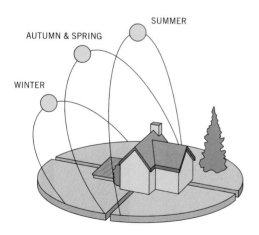

SUMMER

AUTUMN & SPRING

WINTER

The sun crosses the sky in a slightly changing arc every day, affecting the length of shadows.

DEALING WITH RAIN & SNOW If you live in an area that experiences heavy snowfall, your overhead structure must be able to handle the weight. In addition, the effect the structure will have on runoff from rain and snow must be carefully considered.

LEGAL RESTRICTIONS

Contact your local building department to learn about the regulations that apply to outdoor structures in your area.

BUILDING CODES These set minimum safety standards for materials and construction techniques, such as the depth of footings and foundations; the size and type of posts, beams, and other structural members; and requirements for steel reinforcing in foundations.

BUILDING PERMITS Depending on a project's size, whether or not it will be attached to the house, and its intended use, permits are often required. Projects entailing electrical or plumbing may require permits for each task.

ZONING ORDINANCES Ordinances restrict the height of residential buildings, limit lot coverage (the amount of the lot a building or group of buildings may cover), specify setbacks (how close to the property lines you can build), and, in some areas, stipulate architectural design standards.

Though overheads, gazebos, and other garden structures rarely exceed height limitations, they often are affected by setback requirements (see the illustration above). These structures also add to your overall lot coverage, an important consideration if you anticipate adding on to your home in the future.

DRAWING UP A DESIGN

Though most of the projects in this book were designed and built to blend into a very specific setting, many can be modified to suit other needs. For complicated alterations, consider getting some design help.

A good scale drawing will show you how well a roof design is working and how it fits into the house-garden relationship. If you're planning a gazebo or other detached garden shelter, the drawing will enable you to visualize logical traffic patterns, as well as how the size and shape of the structure fits in with your home and yard.

MAKE A BASE MAP Use graph paper to make a base map that shows the physical properties of your lot and house.

Be sure to include the following:

- Dimensions of your lot
- Location of the house, as well as a pool, spa, or any other structures
- Doors and windows and their rooms
- Points of the compass showing how your house is sited
- Path and direction of the sun and any hot spots created
- Utilities (water, gas, and sewer lines) and the depth of each; underground and overhead wires

- Setback lines
- Direction of prevailing winds
- Existing trees and other large plants
- Any obstructions beyond the lot that may affect sun, wind, views, or privacy

EXPERIMENT Using your base map, analyze the best site for your overhead or outdoor structure. Next, place tracing paper over the map and sketch your ideal design. Then, with a scale ruler, calculate what its actual dimensions would be. Go out to the yard and confirm its size and placement, using a tape measure.

ESTABLISHING A BUDGET

As with most building projects, the two main factors determining cost are materials and labor.

Start by selecting your preferred materials, then make changes or

adjustments as your budget dictates.

Even if you have the skills and experience to build your project yourself, keep in mind the value of your time. A professional might be able to accomplish in a few days what would take you a few weeks. Also take inventory of your tool kit. If your project requires several tools you will need to buy or rent, it might be more cost-effective to contract out certain aspects of the project.

Finally, don't forget to add in any fees for special needs and permits. If your site requires the services of a soils engineer, for example, you will need to add that to your budget. If your project includes plumbing or electrical, requiring the services of those professionals, you will not only incur those labor costs but, most often, if those services are required, permits for that work will also be required.

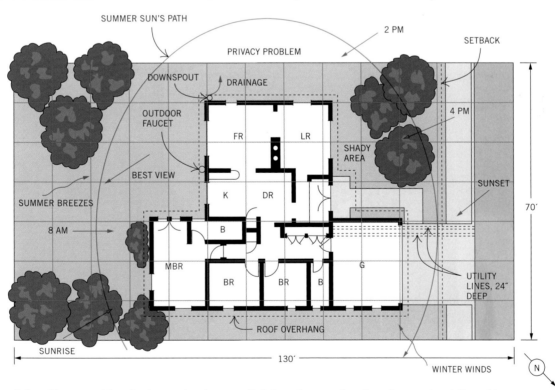

Before siting your outdoor structure, make a base map that shows the properties of your house and yard, then add sun exposures, prevailing wind conditions, views, areas of shade, and areas that lack privacy.

WORKING WITH PROS

Many people who add an overhead or other garden structure seek some professional help at either the design or construction stage. It pays to call a professional for a design that will require engineering, complex components, hard-to-work-with materials, difficult placement on the site, or other aspects that may push designing or building the project beyond your skill set.

To find design professionals or builders, ask friends or neighbors who have had similar work done. Trade associations also can recommend licensed professionals in your area.

DESIGN & BUILDING PROFESSIONALS

Here are some of the professionals who can help you, along with suggestions for working with them:

ARCHITECTS & LANDSCAPE ARCHITECTS These are state-licensed professionals with degrees in architecture or landscape architecture. They're trained to create designs that are structurally sound, functional, and aesthetic. They also know construction materials, can negotiate bids from contractors, and will supervise the work.

LANDSCAPE & BUILDING DESIGNERS These professionals usually have a landscape architect's education and training but are not licensed. Building designers may offer construction help along with design.

DRAFTSPERSONS A draftsperson can create the working drawings required before you can secure building permits and from which you or your contractor can work. Some draftspersons, who are usually less expensive than landscape architects and designers, also may provide designs. If you are modifying a plan in this book, a qualified draftsperson may be all you need.

SOILS & STRUCTURAL ENGINEERS If you're planning to build a structure on an unstable or steep lot or where heavy winds or loads are a consideration, you must consult these specialists.

A soils engineer evaluates soil conditions on a proposed construction site and establishes design specifications for foundations that can resist the stresses unstable soil exerts.

Structural engineers, often working with the calculations a soils engineer provides, design foundation piers and footings to suit the site. They also may provide wind- and load-stress calculations as required.

GENERAL & LANDSCAPE CONTRACTORS These professionals specialize in construction, though some also have design skills and experience. Contractors may do all the work themselves or assume responsibility for hiring quali-

ABOVE: Professional gazebo builders offer stock designs they can then customize to your specifications, eliminating the need for other detailed planning.

LEFT: When building an intricate project— such as this teahouse—on a difficult site, you're likely to need a range of professionals.

fied subcontractors, ordering construction materials, and seeing that the job is completed according to contract.

SUBCONTRACTORS Contractors who specialize in particular areas of construction—electrical, masonry, plumbing, and so forth—are known as subcontractors. If you act as your own general contractor, you'll be responsible for hiring and supervising subcontractors and obtaining permits. When dealing with subcontractors, give them clear instructions, put all agreements in writing, and provide as much direct supervision as possible.

THE PROCESS

At least three working arrangements are open to you if you choose to work with a designer or contractor.

CONSULTATION An architect or landscape architect will review your plans, possibly suggest ideas for a more effective design, and perhaps provide a couple of rough conceptual sketches, working on an hourly basis or day rate.

FEE Another route is to negotiate a flat fee for a given amount of work—for example, to design or modify your project and provide working drawings, with the understanding that you will oversee construction.

PLANNING THROUGH CONSTRUCTION Last, you can retain designers or contractors on a planning-through-construction basis. Besides designing your project the professional will supervise or perform the construction.

You do not necessarily want to choose the contractor who gives you the lowest bid. Base your decision on

Most out-of-the ordinary materials, such as stone and slate, will require specialists—in this case, a stone mason, and most likely a structural engineer due to the weight of the building.

both the individual's reputation (check references carefully) and the bid. Be sure the contractor is someone you feel comfortable with; the person should be well established, cooperative, competent, and financially solvent.

WRITING A CONTRACT

If you hire a contractor to build your garden structure, you'll need a written contract. The more complete the contract, the better the chances that neither the process nor the result will be flawed. It's a good idea to consult a lawyer before signing any agreement for work on your property.

Here are some items you can expect to find in the contract:

CONSTRUCTION MATERIALS All major materials, including hardware, should be identified by quality markings (species, grades, and other quality identifiers) and model numbers where

applicable. Anything not included and added later will increase your costs.

WORK TO BE PERFORMED For example, if you want the contractor to prepare the site, the contract should explicitly identify the tasks: remove fences and shrubs, tear out concrete, grade, and so forth.

TIME SCHEDULE This should include beginning date, completion date, and perhaps interim dates for completion of certain aspects of the job. Your best leverage is a good working relationship with the contractor, as well as the stipulation that the final payment will be withheld until all work is completed.

METHOD OF PAYMENT It is common for either one payment to be made at the beginning and the balance upon completion, or for payment to be made in installments as work progresses.

SELECTING MATERIALS

Most outdoor shelters are built from wood. Generally, the posts, beams, and rafters are made from dimension lumber; wood choices for roofs include boards, lath, battens, plywood, and woven wood.

Of course, materials aren't limited to wood. Other popular roof materials include outdoor fabrics, plastic or glass panels, screening, and solid roofing such as asphalt shingles. Posts can be made from concrete or steel.

The following information will help you choose a material that's appropriate for your project. For information on working with materials, turn to the Tools and Techniques chapter beginning on page 102.

WOOD BASICS

Wood is easy to cut, shape, and fabricate; it comes in a wide range of sizes, from thin lath to large beams, and in many species, grades, and textures. Its workability, variety, and natural appearance make wood an outstanding choice for outdoor construction. For complete information on choosing and buying lumber, see page 104.

LUMBER SIZES Narrow lumber (less than ¾ inch thick) is commonly referred to as either lath or batten. The term "boards" generally denotes lumber that is ¾ or 1 inch thick and more than 2 inches wide. Lumber that's between 2 and 4 inches thick and is at least 2 inches wide is called dimension lumber. Timber is anything larger.

Boards, dimension lumber, and timber are the most commonly used materials for posts, beams, rafters, and open-style roofing. Throughout this book you'll see 1 by 2s, 2 by 4s, 4 by 4s, and other typical sizes used again and again, in many combinations and configurations. To help you decide what types and sizes of wood you will need for your project—and calculate the amounts—see the chart opposite.

Lath is a popular choice for open-style roofing. Strictly speaking, com-

ABOVE: A simple gazebo design is made unique through the use of saw-shaped timbers that have been sandblasted. Though the customized structure looks expensive, all of the timbers employed are cut from standard sizes.

LEFT: Twin arched arbors are testament to the ease with which wood can be shaped. To ensure long life, these structures were carefully stained before assembly and the posts were embedded in substantial concrete piers.

mon outdoor lath is rough-surfaced redwood or cedar that's about ⅜ inch by 1½ inches; it's sold in lengths of 4, 6, and 8 feet, often in bundles of 50. In a broader sense, the term "lath" can refer to any openwork slat roofing.

For outdoor overheads, look for high-quality lath that's free of an excessive amount of knots or other defects. Relatively straight grain is also important to minimize the warping and twisting that can occur due to changing weather conditions.

Batten resembles overgrown lath, milled in thicknesses of ¼ to ¾ inch and in widths of 2 to 3 inches. Batten can be purchased in lengths of up to 20 feet and is generally sold by the piece. In certain regions, smooth-surfaced

batten is called lattice, though the term "lattice" is also used to describe a crosshatch panel of lath material.

LUMBER TEXTURES Milling can produce several different textures. Though surfaced lumber that is smooth is the most familiar, rough or resawn textures are available for a more rustic look.

Surfaced lumber, designated "S4S" ("surfaced on four sides"), is the standard for most construction. You can also buy lumber in all grades that has been planed on one, two, or three sides.

Rough lumber, which has been milled to size but not planed smooth, has rough, splintery surfaces. It tends to be available only in lower grades and with higher moisture content. Though buying rough lumber can save you money, pieces with excessive knots, flat grain, or high moisture content can warp and twist. It can be stained but is a poor choice for painting.

Resawn lumber is wood that has been run through a coarse-bladed saw, such as a band saw, to create a scored texture. Though it isn't stocked at most lumberyards, many landscape professionals special-order resawn lumber

MAXIMUM RAFTER & BEAM SPANS

An essential part of planning your project is determining the number, size, and spacing of rafters, beams, and posts, according to the loads they will carry.

In areas with mild climates, patio roofs are generally designed for loads of 30 psf (pounds per square foot). For heavy roofs or in areas with substantial snowfall or winds, call your local building department for code requirements.

The tables here give maximum recommended spans for rafters and beams. The figures are based on quality materials. For lesser grades, spans should be shorter. Keep in mind that these are maximums—in other words, shortening them slightly will result in a more solid structure.

Find out the loads your overhead must bear, then determine the rafter sizes that will carry the weight. Next, calculate beam placements and how best to coordinate them with the rafters.

MAXIMUM RAFTER SPANS

Rafter Size	Rafter Spacing		
	12″	16″	24″
2 by 4	9′0″	8′3″	7′3″
2 by 6	14′6″	13′0″	11′6″
2 by 8	19′0″	17′0″	15′0″

MAXIMUM BEAM SPANS

Beam Size	Spacing between Beams (or Beam to Ledger)				
	4 feet	8 feet	10 feet	12 feet	16 feet
2 by 6	7′11″	7′0″	6′6″	6′3″	5′6″
2 by 8	10′6″	9′6″	8′6″	8′0″	7′6″
2 by 10	13′4″	12′0″	11′3″	10′6″	9′6″
2 by 12	16′3″	14′6″	13′6″	12′9″	11′6″
4 by 4	6′11″	6′0″	5′6″	5′3″	4′9″
4 by 6	10′10″	9′6″	8′9″	8′3″	7′6″
4 by 8	14′4″	12′6″	11′6″	11′0″	10′0″
4 by 10	18′3″	16′0″	14′6″	14′0″	12′6″
4 by 12	22′2″	19′6″	18′3″	17′0″	15′6″

because of its rustic, but not too rough, texture. It accepts wood stains beautifully and is available in all grades. This is a real plus when higher grades are needed for strength. On the downside, you'll pay a premium for it.

Sandblasted lumber isn't a milled product, but it has a rustic appearance similar to resawn wood. Sandblasting surfaced lumber is generally not cost-effective unless you're having other sandblasting work done (on your pool or siding, for example).

PLYWOOD

In gazebo and patio roof construction, plywood occasionally serves as roof sheathing, to strengthen the structure, or for building concrete forms. Plywood siding occasionally covers gazebo walls or substitutes as a roofing material.

Standard plywood panels measure 4 by 8 feet; thickness ranges from ¼ to ¾ inch. Panels come in interior or exterior grades; specify exterior where plywood will be exposed to the elements.

The appearance of a panel's face and back determines its grade, designated by the letters A through D, A being the highest and D the lowest. Exterior panels graded A/C are economical choices where only one side will be visible. Face and back grades, glue type, and group number should be stamped on each panel, along with an association trademark that assures its quality.

Before using and after cutting plywood, seal all edges with water repellent, stain sealer, or exterior house paint primer to prevent moisture penetration (see page 123).

OTHER WOOD PRODUCTS

Though they don't fit in to standard lumber categories, several other wood products are commonly used in the construction of outdoor overheads. Some are readily available; others require more searching. Many of them are chosen for their openness or to serve as an inexpensive support to flowering vines (see "Vines for Patio Roofs & Gazebos" opposite).

GRAPE STAKES These favorites of fence builders are readily available at garden and lumber supply outlets and offer a hand-hewn look perfect for rustic, open-style roofing. Made from redwood or cedar, they are roughly

ABOVE: A gazebo made from lodge poles topped with a wood-shingled roof fits in seamlessly with its naturally wooded setting.

LEFT: Rustic tree limbs artfully join to create a twist on the classic gazebo. Though not readily available in garden or lumber supply outlets, they can be special-ordered by a landscape architect or contractor.

2 by 2 inches and are usually available in 6-foot lengths. Split grape stakes, more the size of 1 by 2s, also make a satisfactory, rustic-looking overhead.

POLES Bean poles, 1-by-1-inch lengths of redwood or cedar, and preservative-treated lodge poles, vegas (Southwestern-inspired lodge poles), and tree stakes lend a very rustic appearance to an overhead. They're sold by some specialty landscape supply firms.

VINES FOR PATIO ROOFS & GAZEBOS

For many homeowners, an overhead is not just a way to provide shade and dimension to a patio or deck; it is a means to enhance the garden as well. Climbing vines are an integral part of many designs, providing color, lush foliage, fragrance—and shade—seasonally or year-round, depending on where you live.

If such is your desire, your plan should include a watering system that will meet the needs of your plantings yet not deliver water directly on a wood structure. Even so, all posts and beams should be well-treated with a wood preservative to prevent damage.

Following is a list of some of the hardiest vines, by their common names, and then, in parentheses, their scientific names (if different) and the minimum temperatures (in Fahrenheit) that the plants will endure in winter.

ANEMONE CLEMATIS (*C. montana*; −10° F.) This deciduous, fast-growing vine puts on a lavish white to pink floral display in early spring before its leaves emerge. A vigorous climber, its light-green leaves provide moderate to dense shade. It requires light pruning.

BLOOD-RED TRUMPET VINE (*Distictis buccinatoria*; 24° F.) A rapidly growing evergreen vine, this plant blooms brilliantly when the weather is warm; its trumpet-shaped flowers are orange-red fading to bluish red. It provides moderate shade.

BOUGAINVILLEA (30° F.) Though the peak flowering period comes in summer, blooms—in dazzling, neon-bright colors of purple, magenta, crimson, brick red, orange, yellow, pink, or white—may appear from spring through autumn and even into winter in the mildest climates. A fast, vigorous grower with medium-green leaves, this evergreen supplies moderate to dense shade.

CLEMATIS JACKMANII (−20° F.) Though it provides only very light shade, this vine is prized for its large purple flowers, which emerge in summer. Dormant stems must be cut back when new growth starts in the spring.

COMMON WHITE JASMINE (*Jasminum officinale*; 5° F.) This rapidly growing evergreen vine loses some of its foliage in colder regions. Fragrant white flowers bloom throughout the spring. After blooming, the vine must be thinned and pruned to maintain its attractiveness.

EVERGREEN CLEMATIS (*Clematis armandii*; 0° F.) A slow starter, evergreen clematis grows rapidly in warm weather and provides light to moderate shade. Its glossy, dark-green foliage droops downward, creating a strongly textured pattern; flowers, which appear in spring, are fragrant, white, and shaped like stars. After blooming, the plant must be pruned to keep it in check.

GIANT BURMESE HONEYSUCKLE (*Lonicera hildebrandiana*; 20° F.) This plant's dark-green leaves provide moderate shade. Fragrant flowers up to 7 inches long bloom in summer. They are white when they first open, then turn yellow, then soft orange as they age.

GRAPES (American, −25° F.; European, 10° F.) The luxuriant foliage of this deciduous, rapidly growing vine produces dense, cool shade. Fruiting varieties provide edible grapes but may also attract insects.

ROSES (0° F.) Vining roses provide light to moderate amounts of shade and usually grow rapidly. Many varieties are available; choose disease-resistant types with foliage resistant to mildew.

SWEET AUTUMN CLEMATIS (*Clematis dioscoreifolia robusta*; −10° F.) From late summer into autumn, this deciduous vine offers frothy masses of small, fragrant, creamy-white flowers and glossy, dark-green leaves. It grows quite quickly and provides moderate to heavy shade.

WISTERIA (−30° F.) Fragrant, pendulous clusters of white, pink, lavender, or purple flowers characterize this popular vine. The light-green foliage provides moderate to heavy shade.

Part of the planning process for a patio roof or gazebo is considering whether or not you want climbing vines to provide part of your shade.

This structure's plaster walls and vegas blend harmoniously with the home's Southwestern style.

WOVEN REED Readily available at many nurseries and garden supply centers, woven reed comes in 15- and 25-foot rolls that measure 6 feet wide. For durability, it is woven with stainless-steel wire, which can be easily cut and retwisted when the roll is being trimmed to the dimensions of the overhead. Since constant flexing of the wire strands causes them to fail quickly, nail or staple the material to a rigid frame. Reed rolls will last several seasons where protected from rain.

WOVEN BAMBOO Manufactured primarily for vertical-shade use, woven bamboo comes in rolls 3 to 12 feet wide; standard length is 6 feet. Avail-

able in wired form, similar to reed, there are two main grades: split and match stick. Split bamboo is coarser and less regular than match stick, which is made from thin strips of the inner layer of the bamboo stalk. The

split type is preferable for most installations since it's stiffer than match stick, however, match stick is preferred for an adjustable overhead suspended from wires because of its flexibility.

WOVEN SPRUCE & BASSWOOD Similar to woven bamboo, these woods are generally woven with string, but for outdoor use a high grade of seine twine is used.

PREASSEMBLED LATTICE PANELS These panels offer the look of lattice-crisscrossed lath without the work of measuring, cutting, and fastening each piece individually.

Wood lattice panels generally are manufactured in 4-by-8-, 2-by-8-, and 4-by-6-foot sizes. Several grades are available. Only redwood and cedar panels are durable enough for outdoor use. Patterns vary from diagonal or checkerboard designs to variations on these themes.

Resembling carefully painted wood lattice, vinyl lattice panels are smooth, very tough, and never need refinishing. They're also more expensive than

Preassembled lattice panels are a popular choice for shade structures due to their affordability and ease of use.

wood. Vinyl lattice panels are available in white and several earth tones. Typical sheet sizes are 4 by 8 feet, and 2 feet, 10 inches by 8 feet. You can buy panels with diagonal or rectangular lath patterns in different weights and with different lath spacing.

SOLID ROOFING

If you're planning a solid-roof overhead or gazebo, you'll want to consider the roof pitch, or slope, as well as your house's roof, before deciding on a material. (See the section on solid roofing beginning on page 134.)

ASPHALT SHINGLES Asphalt shingles are economical, easy to install and maintain, and are widely available in a broad range of colors, shapes, and specialty patterns. They usually measure 12 by 36 inches.

WOOD SHINGLES Typically made from western red cedar, wood shingles offer natural beauty and durability; they are available in 16-, 18-, and 24-inch lengths. However, they are prohibited in some regions of the country because of fire danger, so check first with your local building department.

WOOD SIDINGS Sidings aren't meant to be watertight, finished-roofing materials, but they can provide serviceable roofing for gazebos and similar structures when pitched for efficient water runoff. You'll need to apply building paper underneath for rain protection and treat the siding (see page 123) to withstand the elements.

The most appropriate milled patterns of solid-board siding for roofing are horizontal shiplap or bevel patterns that shed rain like shingles do. Red-

This stately gazebo features a solid roof made of plywood and vertical battens. Plywood is lightweight and affordable but must be given a very durable finish.

wood and cedar are the most popular species because of their natural resistance to decay. Boards are ¾ inch thick; widths vary from 4 to 12 inches, and lengths run up to 20 feet.

Plywood and hardboard sidings can serve as both roof sheathing and siding. They come in sheets, which cover a large surface quickly, or lap boards. Standard sheet sizes are 4 by 8 feet. Lap boards are 6 to 12 inches wide and 16 feet long. Unfinished varieties must be treated with a durable finish.

OTHER ROOFING MATERIALS Nearly any solid roofing material used on a house can be applied to a patio roof or gazebo, from vinyl and aluminum siding to concrete tiles or built-up roofs. These materials generally require professional planning and installation.

OUTDOOR FABRICS

Canvas and similar fabrics are favored by many for awnings and patio roofs. These fabrics can block or diffuse sun, shed rain, and add color and texture. Their nature allows them to be drawn taut into flat planes, to curve gracefully over vaulted skeletons, or to hang and gather like curtains.

Because these fabrics are lightweight, the supporting structure can often be lightweight as well (though in windy regions they may require engineered framing). Many canvas-style covers also offer the option of being removed when not desired.

The specialty fabrics discussed on the following pages can be found at awning dealers. Look through samples for colors, patterns, and properties that are right for your application.

Colorful, lightweight, capable of deflecting rain and diffusing sun, all with an affordable price tag—these are the attributes that make canvas-style roofing a popular choice. Following are several different ways of making and installing a fabric roof and suggestions on caring for it once it's up.

DESIGN & INSTALLATION The framework that supports fabric is commonly made from pipes, rods, tubing, or wood. Pipes and rods are frequently used because they offer maximum support with minimum visibility. The canvas top can be strapped or laced to the frame, or attached through casings sewn in the fabric that fit the frame.

If you choose not to make the roof yourself, many awning dealers can do it for you. They will work with you to design the fabric's pattern, the framework that will support it, and the method of attachment, then they will sew the pieces together and have a steel frame welded to specification.

MAKING A CANVAS ROOF Most outdoor fabrics typically come in widths of 46 inches, though 60-inch widths are available. Unless your design utilizes single widths, it's likely that pieces will have to be sewn together. If you have the right sewing equipment and skills, you can do it yourself.

Though you can sew 10-ounce duck on most sewing machines, fabric that's vinyl-coated or painted is best entrusted to an awning shop. Canvas heavier than 10-ounce must be sewn with special equipment. (Though you can hand-sew canvas, using a No. 13 sail-

maker's needle, it is arduous work, especially if the cover is large.) If you do sew your own cover, buy the thread from the canvas dealer.

LACING FABRIC ON A FRAMEWORK A typical method of fastening outdoor fabric to a frame is by threading nylon rope or cord through grommets installed around the fabric's perimeter and tying it to the framing members. An awning shop will put the grommets in for you at a minimal charge, or you can buy a simple kit and do it yourself. Either way, make sure the grommets are placed at each corner and every 8 inches along the edges.

If you don't like the look of laced-on canvas, cut the canvas extra long so you can wrap the edges around the frame and lace them together across the top, out of view.

USING CASINGS Another method of attachment is to sew casings, or sleeves, along the edges of the fabric, then slip the frame members through them. This method requires precise measurements or installation may be difficult, tension across the fabric may be irregular, and, over time, the fabric may sag—all adding up to difficulty in repair, maintenance, and storage.

MAKING AN ADJUSTABLE SYSTEM You can make an adjustable overhead by suspending fabric from strong cables. With this system, the fabric can be shifted to cover a certain area and retracted to open up another.

This type of cover is usually made up of a series of 5-foot-wide parallel strips. Wider pieces can be used, but they may be cumbersome to move back and forth on the cables; also, the larger the strips, the more liable they are to sail off in a strong wind.

To make an adjustable cover, attach a stainless-steel cable to the frame with large screw eyes or awning hinges. Add a turnbuckle at one end of the cable to take up slack. Suspend the fabric from rings passed through grommets along the fabric's edges.

MAINTENANCE Outdoor fabrics will last as long as possible with modest but regular maintenance. Keeping them clean is your best guarantee. Don't let dirt, leaves, or other debris accumulate on top—they can cause stains and promote mildew.

Hose the fabric down from time to time, and if possible, sweep it occasionally with a stiff, clean broom. When a more thorough cleaning is required, use a mild, natural soap (not a detergent) and thoroughly rinse it off.

In addition, be very careful about using insecticides or any other chemical sprays near an outdoor fabric; they can cause permanent stains and reduce the fabric's water repellency. Last but not least, never barbecue under a fabric shade—even if you avoid the potential for fire, the damage from smoke can be considerable.

Though not as long-lasting as other overhead materials, outdoor fabric is an affordable and attractive option. This arched roof provides substantial shade to the deck below but does not obscure views or light.

ACRYLIC FABRIC Though acrylic fabric is priced competitively to canvas, it's nearly twice as durable. It's also color-fast, mildew-resistant, and much more apt to stretch than tear. In addition, it sheds rain without leaking.

The man-made fiber, which should last five to ten years, has a soft, woven look and is offered in a broad palette of colors and patterns. Acrylic fabric is translucent, though the degree of opacity varies with the color. On the negative side, since the fabric is woven, colors may not be as crisp as painted-on colors.

Under normal conditions, acrylic won't mildew, unless leaves and debris are left to mildew on top of it. Occasional hosing accompanied by a light brushing to remove dirt, leaves, and twigs will help prolong the fabric's life and maintain its beauty.

Weight is typically 8½ ounces per square yard; fabric width is normally 46 inches, though 60-inch widths are available in some marine grades.

COTTON DUCK Cotton duck (canvas) comes in a variety of solid colors and in stripes. The painted type has a coat of acrylic paint on its weather-facing surface, which makes the duck opaque. However, because the paint has a dull finish, it leaves the linen texture visible; from the underside, you see a pearl green surface. Painted duck may become brittle over time, but with normal maintenance it should last five to eight years.

Dyed duck has color running throughout the fabric. It can be waterproofed to extend its life, but generally it won't last as long as painted duck. Also, because the natural fabric is uncoated, it's more prone to mildew.

In addition to filtering sunlight, screening is a must in humid areas to prevent entry of insects. Most types are made from aluminum or fiberglass and with regular care will last indefinitely.

VINYL-COATED COTTON CANVAS The shiny weather-facing surface of this fabric shows little or no texture. Available in solid colors or stripes (usually white with a primary color), it weathers and cleans well. The opaque, green-colored underside keeps the area beneath cool. Its life span is four to seven years.

VINYL-LAMINATED POLYESTER This fabric sandwiches an open-weave polyester scrim between two layers of painted vinyl. The scrim allows light to pass through, making the area below brighter and warmer than with a solid fabric. Sold in a wide range of solid colors and stripes, the surface has a matte finish and the underside may be either colored or sand white. A good choice for humid areas because it resists mildew, the material should last five to eight years, though the scrim can delaminate if repeatedly folded.

SCREENING MATERIALS

Screening filters sunlight and, when fine meshes are used, prevents entry of insects. A wide array of screening materials is available; the most popular types are made from aluminum or fiberglass and are woven in a mesh of 18 by 16 strands per square inch.

Hardware and home-improvement stores stock some types; for other varieties, check the Yellow Pages under "Screens—Door & Window."

ALUMINUM SCREENING Corrosion-resistant aluminum screening has a long life expectancy under normal conditions; however, like other metals, it will deteriorate in coastal regions. If struck or strained, it tends to bulge rather than break.

Aluminum screening comes in three colors: black, dark gray, and bright aluminum. The darker the color, the better the visibility from inside the structure. It is sold as aluminum window screening in rolls 7 or 25 feet long and 24, 28, 30, 32, 36, and 48 inches wide. (Longer 100-foot rolls may be special-ordered in several widths, from 18 to 72 inches.)

VINYL-COATED FIBERGLASS Strong and lightweight, vinyl-coated fiberglass is the most popular screening material. It won't corrode, rust, oxidize, or stain, but it tears more easily than aluminum and will stretch. Strands of .013 millimeter are recommended for outdoor enclosures such as patio rooms or gazebos. Colors include silver, light and dark gray, and aquamarine.

You'll find fiberglass screening in the same sizes as aluminum, and up to 84 inches wide.

PORCH SCREENING Used for patio, porch, and gazebo enclosures (in addition to conventional window and door screens), tightly woven vinyl-coated fiberglass solar or "sun" screening dramatically blocks heat gain. It utilizes slightly larger, stronger strands than regular fiberglass screening and reduces light transmission by about 30 percent. Standard mesh size is 18 by 14, but in areas where insects are abundant, 20-by-20 mesh is available. Keep in mind, however, that the smaller the mesh, the more light and breezes will be cut down.

During the daytime, solar screen appears almost opaque from outside but offers good visibility from inside. Five colors are available: charcoal, bronze, dark bronze, silver gray, and gold. Charcoal and silver gray are the most commonly available.

PLASTIC MESH One of the best screening materials for use in coastal areas, plastic mesh will not corrode and is unaffected by humidity and salty air. Available by the running foot in widths of 24, 30, 36, 42, 48, and 72 inches, plastic mesh can be ordered by the roll or by the piece. Be aware that the wider the width, the more difficult it may be to pull tight and nail, and the greater the tendency to sag.

ALUMINUM-AND-PLASTIC SCREENING The horizontal wires of this screening hybrid—aluminum coated with plastic—are broad and flat to reduce sun penetration. Colored a neutral gray, the screen is easy to see through from the inside yet affords privacy when viewed from the outside.

PLASTIC & GLASS

Plastic or glass can be an ideal roofing choice when you want protection from rain yet maximum exposure to sunlight and starry skies.

ACRYLIC PLASTIC Acrylic is shatter-resistant, weighs less than glass, and can be transparent or translucent—ideal traits for a roofing material where rain repellency and light transmission are important considerations. In addition, sheets of acrylic are easy to cut, shape, drill, and fasten with fairly standard woodworking tools.

On the negative side, acrylic scratches easily so you may want to

Acrylic plastic is an ideal choice when you want a lightweight roofing material that offers protection from the elements yet allows for the transmission of sunlight.

limit its use to areas away from trees or where scratches will go unnoticed.

Acrylic plastic also comes opaque, in almost every color of the rainbow, but remember that colored plastic will shed colored light.

Thicknesses range from ⅛ to ½ inch. Of course, the thicker the material, the more expensive it is, but the thinner the material, the more support it will require to prevent sagging and the more likely it will be to crack.

To find acrylic-plastic dealers, look under "Plastics—Rods, Tubes, Sheets, Etc." in the Yellow Pages.

POLYESTER RESIN & VINYL Commonly referred to as "fiberglass," these widely used patio roofing materials are often reinforced with fiberglass for added strength. Translucent types are the most popular and come in several patterns: corrugated, flat, crimped, staggered shiplap, and simulated board-and-batten. Opaque corrugated vinyl panels, which block light entirely, are also available.

Standard panel sizes range from 24 to 50½ inches in width and 8 to 20 feet in length. Thickness varies by color and type. Corrugated rolls run 40 inches wide, flat rolls 36 inches wide.

GLASS Because glass is relatively expensive, quite heavy, fragile, and very tricky to work with, it's best to consult a professional if you want to use it. Be advised that in nearly all overhead applications, building codes closely regulate the acceptable types of glass and supporting framework.

POSTS & COLUMNS

Though wood posts are standard for most patio roofs and gazebos, concrete,

Columns are a beneficial post choice when the architectural style of a home calls for them or in situations where added strength is needed. They come in structural and nonstructural types.

steel, and other materials are occasionally used in special situations—to provide added strength or to blend with the style of the house, for example. For more about post materials and designs, see page 124.

ARCHITECTURAL COLUMNS Classic and decorative columns are available through millwork dealers. Structural types are made from wood, aluminum, and fiberglass composites. Nonstructural types, usually designed to conceal a wood or steel post, are made from these same materials or polyurethane. Many types of columns are sold as kits and may be combined with various decorative caps and bases.

CONCRETE & STUCCO COLUMNS Square or rectangular concrete columns are made by pouring concrete into wood forms. Cylindrical fiber tubes are used to form round columns. Stucco columns are constructed from concrete blocks or wood frames that are then stuccoed.

STEEL STRUCTURES Because structural steel is costly it's often reserved for use where extreme loads must be carried over unstable soil. Impervious to fire, rot, and termites, steel posts offer exceptional endurance. Often, steel posts are hidden under a facade of wood. Steel structures must be professionally engineered and fabricated.

step-by-step

TEA ARBOR

This charming arbor is guaranteed to draw you outdoors, whether for tea with a friend . . . or some work on the laptop! The white-painted formal arbor is 80 inches wide, 38 inches deep, and 90 inches tall. It is particularly inviting if tucked into a lushly planted area of the garden. Design: David Snow, English Arbor Company.

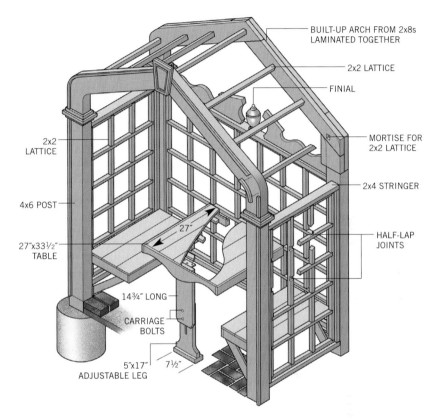

BUILT-UP ARCH FROM 2x8s LAMINATED TOGETHER

2x2 LATTICE

FINIAL

MORTISE FOR 2x2 LATTICE

2x4 STRINGER

HALF-LAP JOINTS

2x2 LATTICE

4x6 POST

27″x33½″ TABLE

27″

14¾″ LONG

CARRIAGE BOLTS

5″x17″ ADJUSTABLE LEG

7½″

DESIGN DETAILS

The floor here is a brick-in-sand installation, but bluestone over stone dust, pea gravel over landscape fabric, or a grade-level deck using pressure-treated lumber would all be appropriate surfaces.

The elegant finial and pediment over the rear trellis, the trimmed arch, and the white-paint finish are all classical elements that formalize the design. None require special woodworking skills or tools—just a portable jigsaw for cutting the arch and pediment. If you want to create your own profile, keep in mind the design relationship between the scrolled profiles of the table apron and the pediment. You can purchase the finial from a mail-order supply house for woodworkers.

projects

BUILDING NOTES

For embedded posts, use only pressure-treated lumber (and only for the posts) specified for "in-ground use." If you want to use redwood or cedar, install post anchors in the footings and shorten the posts to stand on top of the anchors to prevent contact with soil or concrete.

When you laminate the arch, be sure to use waterproof glue, such as polyurethane, and sand well with 120-grit abrasive paper for an invisible (and less vulnerable) joint.

Long pipe clamps come in handy to draw the posts tight against the lattice frames as they are being fastened.

If your storage space is tight, consider attaching the upper portion of the table leg to the apron with carriage bolts and wing nuts so you can disassemble it easily and store it efficiently.

Carefully fill all countersunk screw and nail holes after priming and before top coating. See Tools and Techniques, beginning on page 102, for information on tools and building procedures.

Front Elevation View

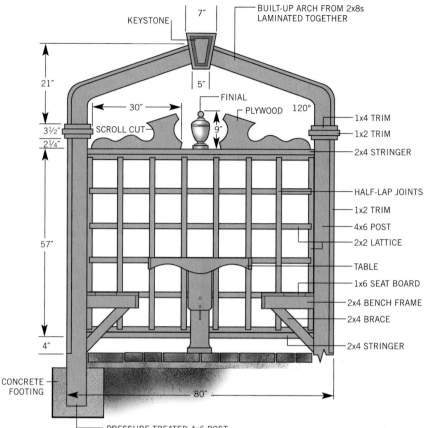

1 Prepare footings for embedded posts as described on pages 120–121, making sure their tops fall below any planned patio or deck. Position the posts and brace them with diagonal braces set between the top of the posts and stakes in the ground. When the concrete has cured, establish a level line across the tops of the posts and cut the posts to length.

2 Rip about $\frac{1}{16}$ inch off the edges of 2-by-8 arch stock to square the edges. Cut the stock for each arch according to the drawing on page 23. Laminate the arch by applying waterproof glue to the two pieces, then connecting with $2\frac{1}{2}$-inch exterior screws.

3 Make a plywood template to guide cutting the rounded forms of the arches. Cut mortises on the inside face of each arch to receive the 2-by-2 roof lattice (see drawing on page 23). Assemble the arches and lattice with construction adhesive and, with at least one helper, position the assembly atop the posts. Bore and countersink diagonal holes for screws through the arch into the posts then fasten the arch in place.

4 Using a router and $\frac{3}{8}$-inch roundover bit, round over the edges of the post-arch assemblies, except the corners on the front face, which will be trimmed.

5 Mill and assemble the two side and rear lattice sections. Using a radial arm saw and dado bit or a circular saw and chisel, cut the half-lap joints in the 2-by-2 lattice stock (see page 23). Toenail the assembly together with galvanized 4d finishing nails.

6 Cut the 2-by-4 stringers to length. Transfer the profile of the detail that will go on top of the rear lattice onto plywood and cut a template. Using the template as a guide, make the scroll cut with a jigsaw. Round over all but the bottom edge with a router and attach to the stringer from the underside with 3-inch screws.

7 Attach the stringers to the top and bottom of each lattice assembly using $2\frac{1}{2}$-inch exterior screws on 6-inch centers. Then install each assembly between

Side Elevation View

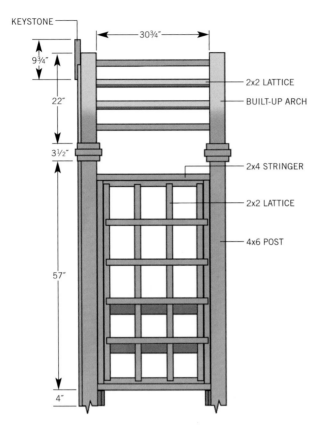

KEYSTONE

9¾"

30¾"

22"

2x2 LATTICE

BUILT-UP ARCH

3½"

2x4 STRINGER

2x2 LATTICE

4x6 POST

57"

4"

Plan View

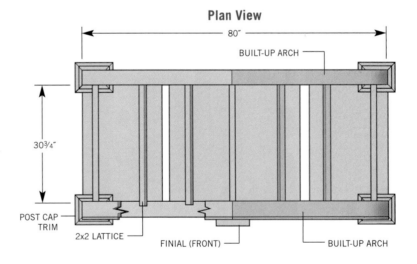

80"

BUILT-UP ARCH

30¾"

POST CAP
TRIM

2x2 LATTICE

FINIAL (FRONT)

BUILT-UP ARCH

the posts and fasten them with screws driven diagonally through the stringers and into the posts.

8 Complete the trim work using galvanized finishing nails. First, trim the post-arch joint, and cut, fabricate, and install the simulated keystone. Then trim the outer edge on the faces of the front and post-arch assemblies. Finally, bore a pilot hole for the finial lag screw and attach the finial.

9 Cut all the parts for both benches. Build the 2-by-4 frame, then attach the 1-by-6 seat and the diagonal braces. Position the assembled bench between the posts, level it, and secure the bench frame and braces to the posts with 2-inch screws.

10 Cut all the parts for the tabletop. Attach the cleat that will support the back edge of the table to the rear trellis with 2½-inch screws. Secure the upper portion of the table leg to the front apron.

Drill pilot holes and cut slots in the lower portion and attach the 2-by-8 square base. Join the two halves with a carriage bolt, washer, and nut. Position the table and adjust the leg height to level.

GAZEBO FROM A KIT

Few outdoor structures equal the charm of a gazebo, but—unless you're a master craftsperson—building an intricate gazebo is well beyond the average do-it-yourselfer's capabilities. Cutting compound angles, shaping wood, making difficult joints are just a few of the tasks involved. Thankfully, several quality woodworking companies produce gazebo kits. With these, most of the difficult work is done—you just provide the spot, assemble the parts, and admire the results. Design: Dalton Pavilions Inc.

BUILDING NOTES

Nearly all gazebo kits come with complete instructions for assembly; be sure to follow them implicitly. The directions given here are for the Dalton Pavilions gazebo shown opposite and on this book's cover. They are specific to this project so they will not be applicable to other models or other manufacturers' gazebos.

With most kits, components are typically numbered or coded to correspond with diagrams and assembly directions. Kits also include screws, bolts, nails, and various connection brackets and plates. Foundation materials are not included.

Because some of the components are heavy or awkward to handle, you'll need a helper. In fact, a large gazebo may require two helpers when it's time to lift the roof components.

Before you begin assembly, you'll need to cast a concrete foundation according to the manufacturer's directions. Proper layout of the foundation piers is critical because the kit's components are sized to fit this layout.

Pour 12-inch concrete piers below grade in accordance with local code requirements. For more about casting a foundation, see the section beginning on page 119.

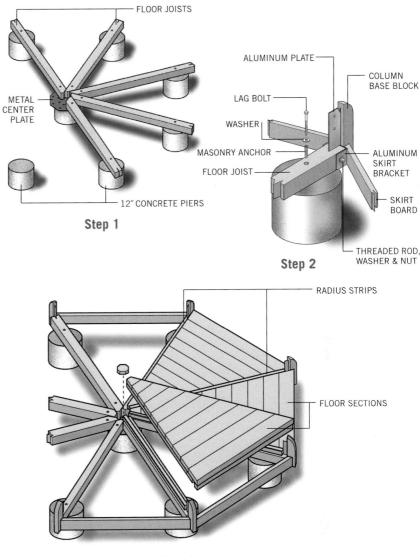

FLOOR JOISTS

METAL CENTER PLATE

12″ CONCRETE PIERS

Step 1

ALUMINUM PLATE

COLUMN BASE BLOCK

LAG BOLT

WASHER

MASONRY ANCHOR

FLOOR JOIST

ALUMINUM SKIRT BRACKET

SKIRT BOARD

THREADED ROD, WASHER & NUT

Step 2

RADIUS STRIPS

FLOOR SECTIONS

Step 3

1 To build the floor framing, first drill-in masonry anchors and lag-screw the metal center plate to the foundation pier at the center of the layout. The octagon's points should be in line with the outer piers. Next, position the eight floor joists and attach them to the center plate using bolts, nuts, and washers. Finger-tighten only. Site down each joist to be sure it lines up straight from its end to the end of the opposite joist.

2 Connect the ends of the joists with skirt boards. Make each connection with a threaded rod, washers, nuts, aluminum skirt brackets, and column base blocks as shown at top right. Be sure the skirt boards' top edges sit flush with the top of the floor joists. Finger-tighten a nut (with washer) at each end of each threaded rod. Now tighten the nuts at the center plate. Then bolt the floor joists to the anchors in the concrete piers using lag screws.

3 To install the floor, line up each section's side edges between two floor joists and place the back edge snug against the column base blocks. Before you screw down the sections, insert radius strips between them, rabbeted edges upward. Using a mallet, tap the floor sections toward the center until the fit is tight and the outer edges of the floor nailers are even. Then use galvanized screws to fasten the floor sections to the joists. Use trim screws to fasten the radius strips to the floor centerpiece.

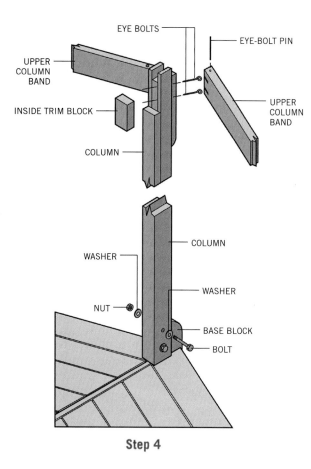

EYE BOLTS

EYE-BOLT PIN

UPPER COLUMN BAND

INSIDE TRIM BLOCK

UPPER COLUMN BAND

COLUMN

COLUMN

WASHER

WASHER

NUT

BASE BLOCK

BOLT

Step 4

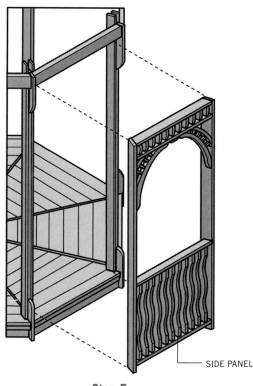

SIDE PANEL

Step 5

4 Using bolts, washers, and nuts, secure the columns to the base blocks, positioning molded sides outward. Attach the upper column bands at the top of the columns using eye bolts and eye-bolt pins. Just finger-tighten the nuts until all of the upper column bands are placed. Then, tighten the nuts, alternating between the right and left nuts on each column. Screw the inside trim blocks in place with trim screws.

5 Install the side panels by positioning each panel so it has equal margins on each side and attaching it to the columns with screws.

6 To install the rafters, start by laying the pair of truss rafters on a flat, level surface and positioning the plastic truss strap straight. Fit the rafter center post between the rafter ends, even with their tops, and secure with screws. With a helper, slide the truss into the slots at the tops of two opposite columns. Be sure the bird's-mouths cut into the rafter ends seat fully and fit against the trim blocks. Then screw the rafters in place. With one person positioned near the center, screw the remaining rafters in place.

7 Depending upon the size of your gazebo, install a roof support band (15-foot model) or a screen band (screened models) between the rafters around the perimeter. Keeping them flush with the top edge of the rafters, screw the bands in place.

8 Center the roof sections over the rafters and secure with screws driven through predrilled holes. Starting at the eaves line, install the hip shingles, starting with a short one, continuing up-roof with long ones, and finishing at the peak with short ones. Secure these with galvanized nails, placing them where they will be covered by the next overlapping shingle.

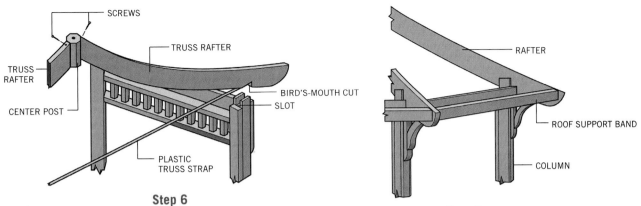

SCREWS

TRUSS RAFTER

TRUSS RAFTER

BIRD'S-MOUTH CUT

CENTER POST

SLOT

PLASTIC TRUSS STRAP

Step 6

RAFTER

ROOF SUPPORT BAND

COLUMN

Step 7

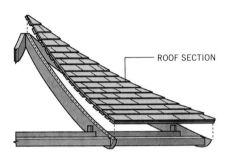

ROOF SECTION

Step 8

PEAK CAP

CUPOLA

THREADED ROD

Step 9

9 Place the peak cap on top so that its threaded rod is projecting up through the cap's center, then screw down the finial, securing it against the peak cap. If you're installing a small cupola on top, use a longer threaded rod and place the cupola's body between the roof and the peak cap.

10 Set any exposed nail heads beneath the surface and fill the holes with matching wood filler. Using a sharp chisel or utility knife, cut and remove the plastic truss strap. If your gazebo comes with open panels, position and fasten the handrails to the columns with screws.

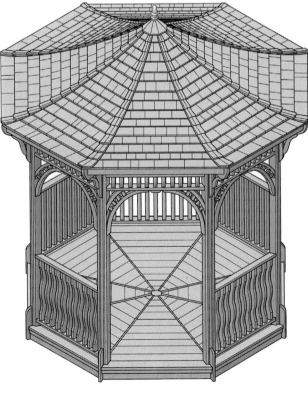

Step 10

CORNER GAZEBO

Elegantly framing the corner of a redwood deck, this charming L-shaped gazebo offers comfortable seating for conversation or quiet contemplation. The white-painted structure has a distinctive hip roof made up of mitered 2 by 2s. Design/Builder: Rex Higbee.

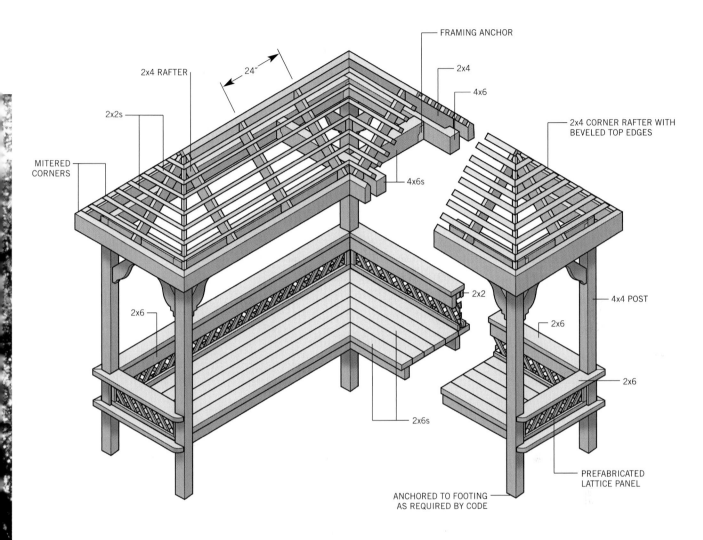

Labels on diagram:
- FRAMING ANCHOR
- 2x4 RAFTER
- 24"
- 2x4
- 4x6
- 2x2s
- 2x4 CORNER RAFTER WITH BEVELED TOP EDGES
- MITERED CORNERS
- 4x6s
- 2x2
- 4x4 POST
- 2x6
- 2x6
- 2x6
- 2x6s
- PREFABRICATED LATTICE PANEL
- ANCHORED TO FOOTING AS REQUIRED BY CODE

DESIGN DETAILS

Built entirely of redwood, this cozy corner gazebo measures approximately 10 feet by 10 feet. The oversized benches are a generous 36 inches deep (that's nearly twice as deep as most outdoor benches) so there's ample room for lounging. Foam seat cushions covered with all-weather fabric add comfort and style. Diagonal-pattern lattice is used across the backs of the benches to create an open, airy feeling. Note: If your lumber dealer doesn't carry redwood in all of the sizes used for this gazebo, you can substitute with other species as long as you paint the unit.

The gazebo's structural frame consists of five 4-by-4 posts, which support 4-by-6 beams. The beams, in turn, support 2-by-4 roof rafters spaced 24 inches on center. The 2-by-2 slats nailed across the rafters are spaced 4 inches on center. This "open roof" design allows some sun to shine through yet provides enough shade to keep the gazebo cool.

MATERIALS CHECKLIST

- 4x4 posts
- 4x6 beams
- 2x4 framing
- 2x4 rafters & fascia
- Prefabricated lattice panels
- 2x2 trellis stock
- 2x6 bench framing
- 2x8 braces
- Galvanized nails & outdoor screws
- Metal post anchors
- Metal framing brackets & fasteners
- Sanding & finishing supplies
- Paint, stain, or wood preservative

BUILDING NOTES

Adding this gazebo to an existing deck requires passing the five posts through the decking and setting them on concrete footings. If the gazebo is part of a new deck plan, reinforce the understructure framing with additional posts and double joists, then fasten the gazebo posts directly to the deck's framing with carriage bolts.

To save time and create strong, solid joints, join together the timbers of the 4-by-6 frame that supports the roof rafters with metal framing anchors.

See Tools and Techniques, beginning on page 102, for complete information on tools and building procedures.

1 If adding the gazebo to an existing deck, first remove the boards where you want to build the gazebo. Mark the locations of the five posts. Dig 12-inch-diameter holes and pour concrete footings for the posts, as described on pages 120–121. Set a metal post anchor into each footing and allow the concrete to cure overnight. Cut the posts to length, adjust for plumb, and attach them to the anchors with galvanized screws. Replace the decking, cutting the boards to fit tightly around the posts.

If the gazebo is part of a new deck plan, fasten the posts to the fortified understructure framing with ½-inch-diameter galvanized carriage bolts.

2 Cut the 4-by-6 beams to span the distance from post to post. Wherever two beams meet, fasten them together with metal framing anchors.

3 Next, cut the 2-by-4 roof rafters to size. Notch each one with a bird's-mouth cut where it rests on top of the beams. Space the rafters 24 inches on center and fasten them with 8d galvanized finishing nails.

Note that the top edges of the hip rafters at the corners of the roof must be beveled at a 45-degree angle to accept the 2-by-2 slats.

Partial Section Elevation

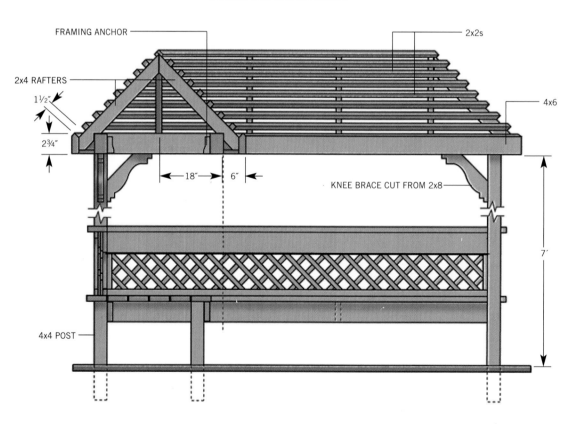

FRAMING ANCHOR

2x2s

2x4 RAFTERS

1½"

2¾"

4x6

18"

6"

KNEE BRACE CUT FROM 2x8

7'

4x4 POST

Plan View

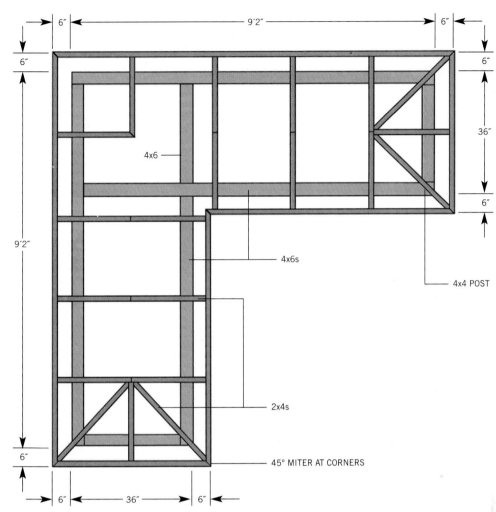

4 Cut 2 by 4s for the fascia. Bevel the top edges of the boards to 45 degrees, then nail them to the ends of the rafter tails. Run the 2-by-4 fascia around the entire roof frame.

5 Install the 2 by 2s across the rafters, starting near the fascia and working up the roof. Cut miter joints at the corners and fasten the 2 by 2s with 10d galvanized finishing nails.

6 From 2-by-8 stock, cut the 10 diagonal knee braces that fit into the corners formed by the posts and beams. Create the decorative scroll-cut pattern

with a sabre saw or band saw (use one piece as a template for marking the others). Fasten the braces to the beams and posts with 3-inch decking screws.

7 Build the bench frame out of 2 by 6s and screw it to the posts. Cut prefabricated lattice panels into 12-inch-wide strips and sandwich them between 2-by-2 cleats nailed to the bench frame.

8 Cover the upper edge of the lattice panels with 2 by 6s to create the railing along the tops of the benches. Carefully notch the 2 by 6s to fit snugly around the posts.

9 Cut 2 by 6s for the bench seats. Note that the boards meet in the corner at 45 degrees. Fasten the boards with 10d galvanized finishing nails, leaving a 1/8-inch space between each one. Tap the nailheads well below the surface with a hammer and nailset.

10 Use an orbital sander to round all sharp corners and smooth all rough surfaces. Pay particular attention to the areas around the benches, railings, and posts. Wipe off the dust and apply a stain-blocking sealer and one or two coats of paint.

ROMANTIC GAZEBO

This irresistibly charming gazebo features lacy latticework arches and railings and a steep-pitched cedar roof. It's built on a concrete slab beside a flower garden and provides a shaded, tranquil place to read, relax, or dine.

Measuring nearly 10 feet across, this octagonal structure can easily accommodate a large table and four chairs, yet it's compact enough to fit into even a modest-size yard. Note that this gazebo features a traditional open-air design, but it could easily be screened in for insect-free nighttime use.
Design: Gazebo Nostalgia.

DESIGN DETAILS

The eight gazebo "walls" are framed with 4-by-4 posts; horizontal 2-by-6 rails frame the base. The lattice archways are trimmed at the top with 2 by 2s and along the bottom edges with 1 by 6s and ⅜-inch-thick redwood benderboard. Prefabricated lattice panels fill in between the framing members.

Each of the eight 4-by-4 posts supports a 2-by-6 roof rafter that's made up of two parts. The main rafter extends at a 45-degree angle from the center hub at the roof peak down to a post. A 2-by-6 rafter tail is attached to the rafter at a 15-degree angle. The two parts are joined together with half-lap joints and machine bolts.

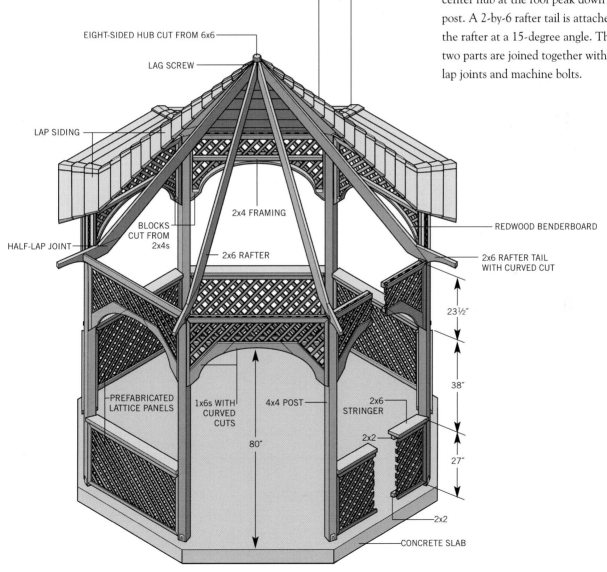

CEDAR HIP SHINGLES

EIGHT-SIDED HUB CUT FROM 6x6

LAG SCREW

LAP SIDING

2x4 FRAMING

BLOCKS CUT FROM 2x4s

HALF-LAP JOINT

2x6 RAFTER

REDWOOD BENDERBOARD

2x6 RAFTER TAIL WITH CURVED CUT

23½"

38"

PREFABRICATED LATTICE PANELS

1x6s WITH CURVED CUTS

4x4 POST

2x6 STRINGER

2x2

80"

27"

2x2

CONCRETE SLAB

Interestingly, the roof is made up of cedar-bevel siding, not shingles. The 6-inch-wide siding is nailed across the rafters, then shingles are used to conceal the joints between the lengths of the siding.

BUILDING NOTES

The reinforced concrete slab should be at least 6 inches thick and 4 inches larger in diameter than the gazebo. If you don't feel confident working with concrete, hire a mason for this part of the project. Another option is to build an octagonal wood deck for the gazebo.

If you're planning to paint the wooden parts, do as much painting as possible before assembling the gazebo. The easiest way to paint lattice panels is with a spray gun.

See Tools and Techniques, beginning on page 102, for complete information on tools and building procedures.

1 Cut the eight 4-by-4 posts to 88½ inches long. Then fully assemble four wall sections (though not the one with the entryway). Join each pair of posts with horizontal 2 by 4s and 2 by 6s. Install the lattice panels between the posts, securing them to the 2-by-2s. Cut the lattice arch to fit between the posts and trim the bottom edges with 1 by 6s and redwood benderboard.

2 Stand one of the assembled wall sections on the concrete slab, just to the left of the entryway location. Position it about 2 inches from the edge of the slab, then check it for plumb and support it in place with a temporary diagonal brace staked to the ground. Secure the posts to the concrete with metal brackets, screws, and lead anchors. Install the three remaining walls, leaving an open wall space between each one.

3 Enclose the spaces between the four standing walls by installing the lattice panels, 2-by-6 rails, and 2-by-2 cleats. Create the entryway by installing the archway lattice. Then trim the bottom of the arch with benderboard.

4 Cut eight long roof rafters and eight short rafter tails from 2-by-6 stock. Join the tails to the rafters with half-lap joints, as illustrated opposite. The easiest way to cut the joints is with a portable circular saw. Set the blade to ¾ inch deep

MATERIALS CHECKLIST

- **Concrete, #4 rebar & form lumber for slab**
- **4x4 posts**
- **6x6 center hub**
- **2x4 framing**
- **2x6 rafters & rails**
- **1x6 trim**
- **2x2 cleats**
- **Prefabricated lattice panels**
- **Redwood benderboard**
- **Cedar bevel siding**
- **Cedar shingles & nails**
- **Silicone sealant**
- **Galvanized nails & outdoor screws**
- **Galvanized machine bolts, washers & nuts**
- **Expansion anchors**
- **Metal post anchors**
- **Sanding & finishing supplies**
- **Paint, stain, or wood preservative**

Elevation View (Frame Only)

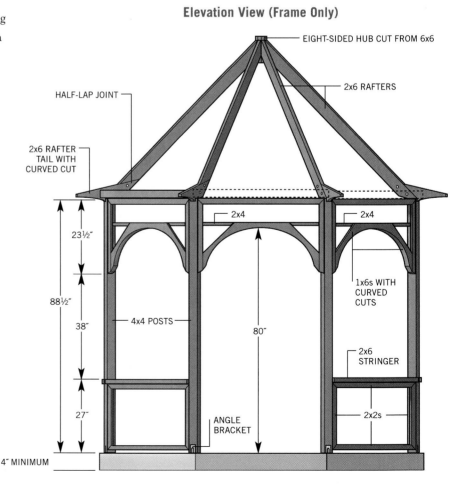

EIGHT-SIDED HUB CUT FROM 6x6

2x6 RAFTERS

HALF-LAP JOINT

2x6 RAFTER TAIL WITH CURVED CUT

2x4

2x4

1x6s WITH CURVED CUTS

23½"

88½"

38"

27"

4x4 POSTS

80"

2x6 STRINGER

2x2s

ANGLE BRACKET

4" MINIMUM

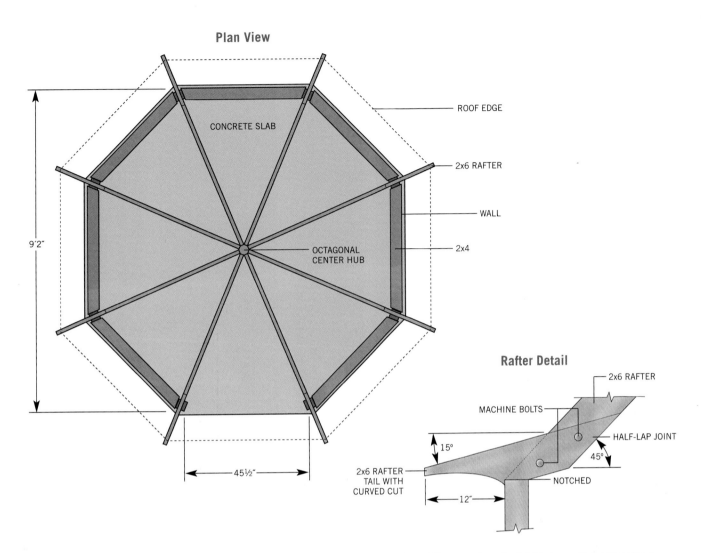

Plan View

ROOF EDGE

CONCRETE SLAB

2x6 RAFTER

WALL

9'2"

OCTAGONAL
CENTER HUB

2x4

45½"

Rafter Detail

2x6 RAFTER

MACHINE BOLTS

HALF-LAP JOINT

15°

45°

2x6 RAFTER
TAIL WITH
CURVED CUT

NOTCHED

12"

and cut away the waste wood from each mating board with multiple cuts, then use a wood chisel to remove waste wood. Fasten the tails to the rafters with galvanized machine bolts and nuts.

5 Make an eight-sided center hub for the roof peak from a 12-inch-long piece of 6 by 6. Use a table saw with the blade tilted to 45 degrees to trim off the corners from the 6 by 6 and form the octagon shape.

6 With a couple of helpers, lift the first rafter into place. Set the lower end on top of a post and secure it with 3-inch decking screws. Hold or brace up the

rafter to keep it from falling, and install the rafter opposite. Slip the octagonal center hub between the two rafters at the peak, then secure the rafters to the hub with 3-inch decking screws. Install the remaining rafters in a similar manner.

7 Begin laying the cedar-bevel siding for the roof at the rafter tails and work your way up to the peak. Cut the siding to span from the center of one rafter to the center of the next. Bore pilot holes in the ends of the siding to prevent splitting, and attach with galvanized siding nails.

8 Use a caulking gun to apply a thick, continuous bead of silicone sealant

along the joint between the siding pieces. The bead should extend from the center hub all the way down to the rafter tails.

9 Conceal the caulked joint along the rafters with cedar shingles. Cut the shingles so they overlap the siding by at least 4 inches on each side of the joint and alternate the lapping edge from one course to the next. Secure the shingles to the roof with shingle nails. Again, be sure to bore pilot holes to prevent splitting. Position the nails so they go through the shingles and siding and into the 2-by-6 rafters below.

10 Sand any rough edges or corners and touch up with paint.

REDWOOD CABANA

With its overhanging hipped roof, this substantial 12-by-12 cabana provides more than 300 square feet of shade. Such a massive structure might overpower an elevated deck but is a perfect shade shelter for a large grade-level deck, a concrete or brick patio, or a spacious yard or garden. Designer/Builder: James Michael Bradbury.

DESIGN DETAILS

The heavy timbers, including 6-by-6 columns (instead of the more typical 4-by-4 posts), 6-by-12 arches, and 4-by-6 corbeled rafters, produce a sturdy cabana/shade shelter that is proportionate to its overall dimensions and in scale to its spacious location on a concrete and brick pool patio.

The roof eaves on the 10-foot tall, 12-foot-square structure extend nearly 3 feet past the columns and 7½ feet above the ground to maximize shade for this large sunny patio.

The choice of redwood and the detailing, such as the fluted columns, steel crown, and eased corners, serve to soften and add character to the structure. The 2-by-6 tongue-and-groove roof decking provides substantial support for any roofing material choice or can be finished naturally.

BUILDING NOTES

Not every lumberyard will have the timbers specified, so you may have to call around. If possible, hand pick your lumber, especially the 6-bys for the four columns and arched beams. Avoid timbers with large knots or that are center cut as these tend to twist or warp.

The 6-by-12 beams are made from construction-grade timbers and need to be surface planed.

The best way to cut the large radius on the arched beams is with a portable band saw. For drilling, you'll need extra-long drill bits or an extension. Depending on the type of lumber, its moisture content, and the number of able-bodied helpers available, you may need a crane, pump jacks, or similar equipment to lift and control the heavy beams as they are hoisted onto their supports. These specialty tools are

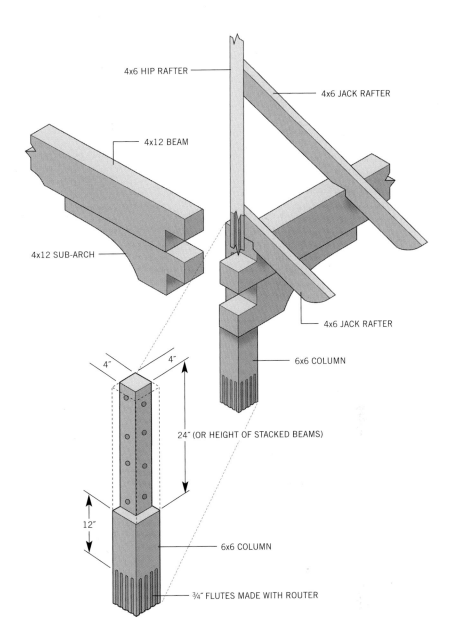

4x6 HIP RAFTER

4x6 JACK RAFTER

4x12 BEAM

4x12 SUB-ARCH

4x6 JACK RAFTER

6x6 COLUMN

4″   4″

24″ (OR HEIGHT OF STACKED BEAMS)

12″

6x6 COLUMN

¾″ FLUTES MADE WITH ROUTER

available at building-supply companies.

At the apex of this structure is a custom-fabricated 3/16-inch steel crown, prepainted with epoxy to prevent rust. The steel crown is expensive to have welded but it eliminates complex compound miter cuts and provides a much stronger connection.

Wherever possible, use through-bolts rather than lag screws, which can loosen over time. Coat them with a good epoxy enamel to prevent rust,

which can stain the beautiful wood. Because this structure involves fairly intricate joinery and heavy, expensive materials, it isn't for every do-it-yourselfer. Be sure you have the appropriate tools and skills before tackling it. Otherwise, call a professional contractor. We recommend that you use these plans and directions as a starting point, adjusting them to suit your site and choice of materials. See Tools and Techniques on page 102.

MATERIALS CHECKLIST

- **Concrete, #4 rebar & form lumber for footings**
- **6x6 columns**
- **4x12 beams**
- **6x12 beams**
- **4x6 rafters**
- **2x6 tongue-and-groove roof decking**
- **Custom-fabricated steel crown**
- **Galvanized nails & outdoor screws**
- **Galvanized machine bolts, washers & nuts**
- **Expansion anchors**
- **6x6 metal post anchors**
- **Sanding & finishing supplies**
- **Paint, stain, or wood preservative**

1 Form and pour the footings (see pages 120–121), which must be at least 24 by 24 by 24 inches to support the weight of the massive structure. Reinforce with No. 4 rebar. Embed post anchors in each footing to accept the columns. To prevent excessive moisture absorption through the end grain, make sure the posts do not sit on the concrete.

2 Cut the columns to their 8-foot, 2-inch length and mill the top 2 feet to 4 by 4 inches to create a shoulder. Using a router and half-round bit, flute 6-inch wide faces on each column, ending 12 inches from each end. Bolt the columns to the post anchors and brace them plumb.

3 Place each long 6-by-12 beam upside down on flat ground. Tack one nail into the top of each beam near the edge face, at the beginning and end points of the curve. Attach a string to the nails and let it drape down about 4 inches along the face of the beam. Trace the curve it makes with a marking pen.

4 Cut the radius on the arches with a portable band saw and cut matching curves at the ends of the sub-arches. Cut a 6-inch notch out of either the top or bottom of each beam end (according to which side of the structure it will be on) to form the half-lap joint that will connect the beams. Note: Measure the actual width of your beams before cutting notches.

5 Similarly, mark and cut the arch and notches on the ends of the sub-arch members. Clamp each member in place atop the shoulders on the columns so you can bore and countersink the mounting holes. Take care to stagger their locations on adjoining sides. Secure the sub-arches with machine bolts, washers, and nuts.

Elevation Section View

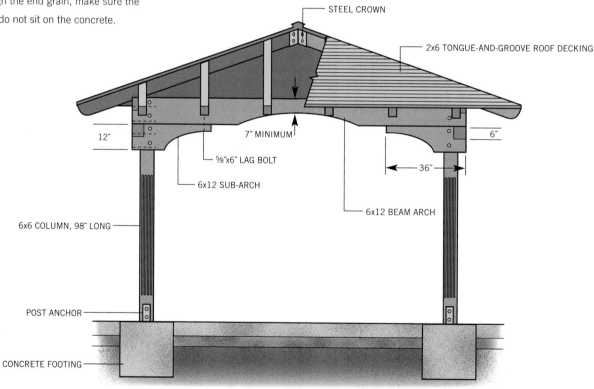

STEEL CROWN

2x6 TONGUE-AND-GROOVE ROOF DECKING

12″

7″ MINIMUM

6″

⅝″x6″ LAG BOLT

36″

6x12 SUB-ARCH

6x12 BEAM ARCH

6x6 COLUMN, 98″ LONG

POST ANCHOR

CONCRETE FOOTING

Plan View (Framing Only)

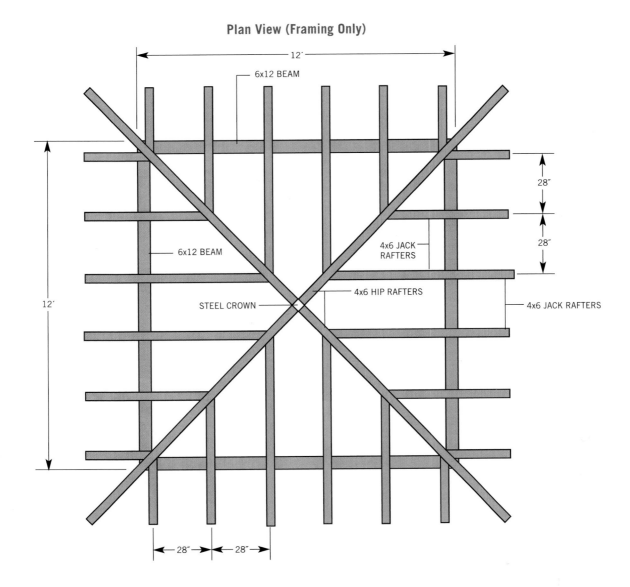

6 Cut a bird's-mouth notch in each hip rafter to fit over the beam; then cut the angle at the top where the four hip rafters fit into the steel crown. Attach them to the beam with lag bolts driven down into the beam, and join the rafters at the apex by bolting them to the steel crown.

7 Cut bird's-mouths in the jack rafters where they rest on the beams and compound angles where they meet the hip rafters. Fasten each pair of jack rafters with machine bolts that extend through all three rafters.

8 Rip the groove off the first course of 2-by-6 decking. Starting at the eaves and working upward, attach the decking using two 3½-inch exterior screws at each connection point. Do one roof plane at a time. Run both ends wild on the first plane, then cut them all to length at once, guided by a snapped chalk line. On the next two planes, cut a compound miter on one end and let the other end run wild. On the last plane, cut compound miters on both ends before fastening.

9 Apply the roofing material of your choice over this base in accordance with the manufacturer's instructions, standard building practices, and local codes. Depending on your choice, underlayment, cedar breather, additional strapping, or other installation materials may be required.

10 Perform any final sanding that may be required. Apply an exterior clear finish or stain suitable for the wood to enhance its appearance and protect it from the elements.

SIMPLE SQUARE GAZEBO

This owner-built 8-foot-square trellis, floored with flagstone and furnished with comfortable chairs, provides an inviting place to relax and enjoy the view from a hillside garden. Without a doubt, this handsome structure also enhances the view of the garden from the house. Landscape architect: Lankford Associates.

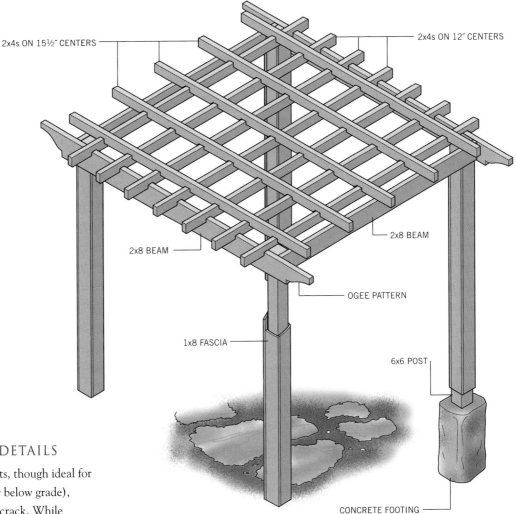

2x4s ON 15½" CENTERS

2x4s ON 12" CENTERS

2x8 BEAM

2x8 BEAM

OGEE PATTERN

1x8 FASCIA

6x6 POST

CONCRETE FOOTING

DESIGN DETAILS

Pressure-treated posts, though ideal for durability (especially below grade), inevitably check, or crack. While checking does not affect strength, it is particularly unsightly when the wood is painted. Capping the posts with boards more suitable for painting, such as better grades of pine or redwood, gives this structure the benefits of both types of wood. In addition, the fascia provides a ledge for the 2-by-8 beams, effectively eliminating the need for bolted connections.

The architectural details at the ends of the front and rear beams can be adapted to blend with design elements of your home. Before cutting the beams, experiment with shaped plywood patterns tacked onto the ends of uncut 2-bys.

BUILDING NOTES

Cut the posts in place after erecting them. Lay out the positions of the crossing 2-by-4 trellis pieces, then mark the tops of the lower ones for the overlapping top ones. Cut the fascia boards so they will end a couple of inches above a patio and even more above soil or plants. After cutting the posts' 1-by-8 fascia boards, soak the ends in a wood preservative to protect the end grain from moisture damage.

To install the two side beams, tack cleats onto posts 7¼ inches down from the top.

MATERIALS CHECKLIST

- Concrete, #4 rebar & form lumber for footings
- Gravel
- 6x6 posts, pressure-treated
- 2x8 beams
- 2x4 trellis stock
- 1x8 trim
- Galvanized nails & outdoor screws
- Sanding & finishing supplies
- Paint, stain, or wood preservative

Cut the notches in the trellis 2 by 4s with a jigsaw, using the first board as a template for the others; or, clamp the 2 by 4s side by side for gang cutting with a circular saw.

Prime all the cut lumber before installing. Use a drum sander or sanding attachment to smooth the end grain of the ogee cuts on the long beams. Countersink nails and fill the holes with exterior filler prior to applying the finish coat.

See Tools and Techniques, beginning on page 102, for complete information on tools and building procedures.

1 Lay out the post locations using batter-boards and string (see page 119) so that the outside dimension of each "side" is 94½ inches. Measure for equal diagonal dimensions to verify the structure will be square. Mark the batterboards.

2 Dig holes for the footings. Set each post on about 3 inches of gravel at the bottom of each hole. Hold the posts plumb with diagonal braces at right angles to each other. Pour the footings (see page 120 for detailed instruction).

3 Using a level and an 8-foot-long straight board, or a water level, mark the tops of the posts at 8 feet, 2½ inches. Clamp or tack a saw guide to the posts to assure a safe and accurate cut with a circular saw. Be very careful when cutting from the top of a ladder.

4 Cut the two long beams to length and cut the ogee detail. Make a template for the ogee detail by using a jigsaw and ¼-inch plywood or similar scrap and clamp it onto the beams to guide your cuts. Lay out the tops of the beams for the 12-inch-on-center 2 by 4s. Secure them with exterior nails or screws.

Elevation View

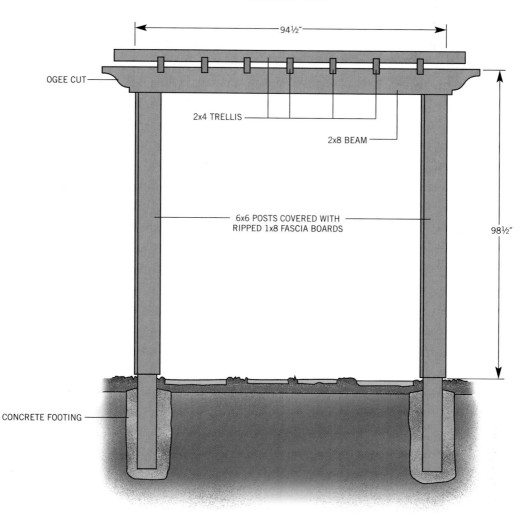

94½"

OGEE CUT

2x4 TRELLIS

2x8 BEAM

6x6 POSTS COVERED WITH
RIPPED 1x8 FASCIA BOARDS

98½"

CONCRETE FOOTING

Plan View

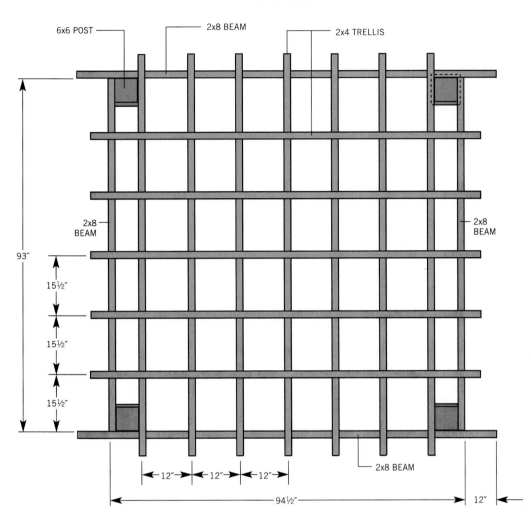

6x6 POST

2x8 BEAM

2x4 TRELLIS

2x8 BEAM

2x8 BEAM

93"

15½"

15½"

15½"

2x8 BEAM

12" 12" 12"

94½"

12"

5 Cut the two side beams to length—equal to the outside post-to-post distance—then secure the beams flush to the post tops with exterior nails or screws.

6 For each post, rip two fascia boards that are about ³⁄₁₆ inch wider than the posts and two that are 1½ inches wider than these.

7 Cut a ¾-by-7¼-inch notch at the top of one inside-corner fascia board for each post so it will fit around the beam. Nail the two outside-corner boards together, then secure them to the posts; do the same for the inside-corner boards.

8 Cut the lower 2-by-4 trellis members to length. Lay one across the top of the long beams on one end, center it for an equal overhang on each end, and mark the 1-by-1½-inch notches where it crosses the two beams. Use this piece as a template for cutting notches in the other 2 by 4s that run this direction.

9 Cut the top 2-by-4 trellis members to length. Locate and cut the notches in the bottoms of them as you did for those in the first course. Predrill pilot holes, then toenail them onto the tops of the first course of trellis.

10 Sand the fascia and ease the corners to eliminate any splinters. Touch up the primer as needed and top-coat the entire structure with 100 percent acrylic latex paint.

HILLSIDE GAZEBO

Perched on the edge of a hillside, this redwood gazebo is accessed by a bridge that connects it to a formal garden with fountain. The beautiful trellis roof filters sunlight to the structure's 100-square-foot interior. Landscape architect: R.M. Bradshaw & Associates.

DESIGN DETAILS

Located as it is on a steep hillside, the gazebo captures outdoor living space that would otherwise be unusable. Though the structure would work with many types and designs of flooring, the redwood planks laid in an octagonal pattern to mirror the roof lend a finishing touch. The decorative facade between the posts just below the roof beams helps to anchor the roof, generally contributes to a sense of shelter and privacy, and serves to support flowering vines. The copper-clad cupola hides the steel center hub ring and is an important focal point.

The relatively wide spacing of the 2-by-2 lattice (6 inches on center) is suitable for mild climates. The wider spacing was also chosen because it is visually interesting when viewed from above, and the home's main living area is on the second floor overlooking the garden. For more shade in a hot climate, simply tighten the spacing.

BUILDING NOTES

Perhaps the single most important step to get right when building a gazebo is making sure the post anchors are precisely positioned. Doing so starts with careful layout, requires that the anchors be braced until the concrete sets up, and, if required, shaving a post to adjust its position before proceeding.

Framing brackets—either those designed to be bent to a desired angle or those already skewed to angles typically encountered when framing octagons—are easier to use than fasteners alone and provide a stronger connection. Galvanized screws and bolts are used throughout.

Decking is spaced according to the

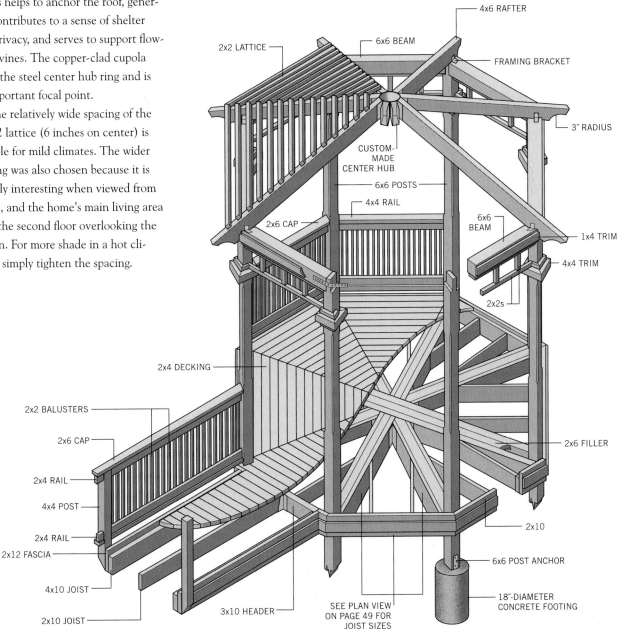

- 4x6 RAFTER
- 6x6 BEAM
- 2x2 LATTICE
- FRAMING BRACKET
- 3" RADIUS
- CUSTOM-MADE CENTER HUB
- 6x6 POSTS
- 4x4 RAIL
- 2x6 CAP
- 6x6 BEAM
- 1x4 TRIM
- 4x4 TRIM
- 2x2s
- 2x4 DECKING
- 2x2 BALUSTERS
- 2x6 CAP
- 2x4 RAIL
- 4x4 POST
- 2x4 RAIL
- 2x12 FASCIA
- 4x10 JOIST
- 2x10 JOIST
- 3x10 HEADER
- SEE PLAN VIEW ON PAGE 49 FOR JOIST SIZES
- 2x6 FILLER
- 2x10
- 6x6 POST ANCHOR
- 18"-DIAMETER CONCRETE FOOTING

lumber species used—in the case of redwood, about ¼ inch apart. The floor structure, which is not visible, is framed with Douglas fir, a species prized for its strength and less costly than redwood. The straps, especially important in earthquake-prone regions, tie the floor system together.

See Tools and Techniques, beginning on page 102, for complete information on tools and building procedures.

1 Make forms and pour eight 18-inch-diameter concrete-pier footings as described on pages 120–121. Embed 6-by-6 post anchors in the wet concrete and brace in position until the concrete cures and the posts are ready to be installed.

2 When the concrete has cured, measure and cut the posts. Notch the tops to create shoulders for the beams to rest on and, using a router, mill a ¾-inch radius at each post corner. Sand with 120-grit paper before installing the posts.

3 Lay the floor next. Secure each pair of radiating joists to the sides of the posts with machine bolts. The metal straps are screwed onto the first layer of the perimeter joists to tie the corners together. Add 2-by-6 fillers between paired joists. Install the 2-by-4 decking with exterior screws.

4 Cut the beams to identical lengths and miter the ends. Position the beams and attach to the posts with screws driven at an angle. Screw two steel straps into the faces of the beams to tie them at the posts.

5 Lay out the rafters and cut them to length, with 30-degree angles at top and bottom. Cut a 3-inch radius on the tails using a jigsaw or band saw. Test fit, then sand all pieces with 120-grit paper.

Install them using framing brackets at the beams and set into hangers welded to the center hub.

6 Trace the center hub's outside dimension onto a 2-by wood block so the cupola can be built and clad off site. Tack the mitered posts to the template, centering them on each of the eight sides. Cut the roof planes from 2-by-6 stock, then glue and screw them together and copper clad the top. Angle screw the posts into the underside of the roof. Clad and install the 1-by-2 trim. Remove the template and install the cupola with screws driven through the posts into the rafters.

7 Sand the 2-by-2 lattice with 120-grit paper before cutting. Then, starting at the cupola, mark the lattice layout 6 inches on center, on the tops of the rafters. Install the lattice with exterior screws. Avoid splitting or splintering the 2 by 2s; bore pilot holes and countersink the screws.

8 Install the 1-by-4 trim on the outside face of the beams to conceal the strapping. Cut and assemble the 2-by-2 components for the decorative facade just under the beams, then install it with galvanized finishing nails. Install the mitered 4-by-4 and 2-by-2 capital trim around the posts below the facade.

Elevation View

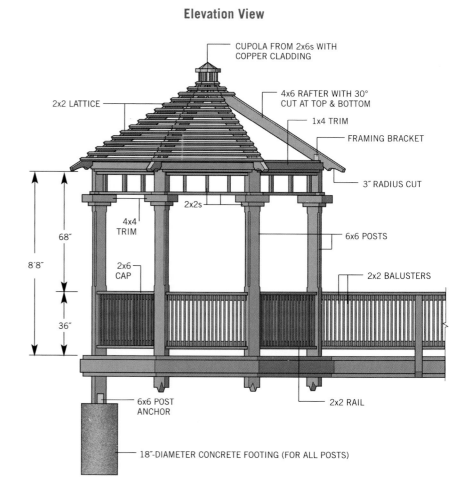

CUPOLA FROM 2x6s WITH COPPER CLADDING

4x6 RAFTER WITH 30° CUT AT TOP & BOTTOM

1x4 TRIM

FRAMING BRACKET

2x2 LATTICE

3" RADIUS CUT

2x2s

6x6 POSTS

4x4 TRIM

2x2 BALUSTERS

68"

8'8"

2x6 CAP

36"

2x2 RAIL

6x6 POST ANCHOR

18"-DIAMETER CONCRETE FOOTING (FOR ALL POSTS)

9 Sand all members with 120-grit paper. Cut and assemble each railing section by attaching 1-by-2 balusters to the wide faces of 2-by-4 rails cut to rough length. Make the final cuts so the spacing between the end balusters and the posts will be equal. Cut and install the bottom flat rail, install the baluster assembly, and finally, mill, cut, and install the 2-by-6 cap.

10 With the construction complete, make sure all fasteners are flush with or set just slightly below the surface and then do a final sanding, especially on any areas within easy reach or close view. Then apply a protective finish such as a semi-transparent stain to minimize the effects of weathering.

MATERIALS CHECKLIST

- Concrete, #4 rebar & form lumber for footings
- 6x6 posts & beams
- 2x6 fillers
- 2x10 joists
- 2x12 fascia
- 3x10 joists & headers
- 4x10 joists
- Custom-fabricated steel center hub
- 2x4 framing
- 4x6 rafters
- 2x2 trellis stock & trim
- 1x2, 1x4, 2x2 & 4x4 trim
- 1x2, 2x4 & 2x6 railing members
- Galvanized nails & outdoor screws
- Galvanized machine bolts, washers & nuts
- Expansion anchors
- Metal post anchors
- Metal framing brackets & fasteners
- Copper finial, flashing & nails
- Sanding & finishing supplies
- Paint, stain, or wood preservative

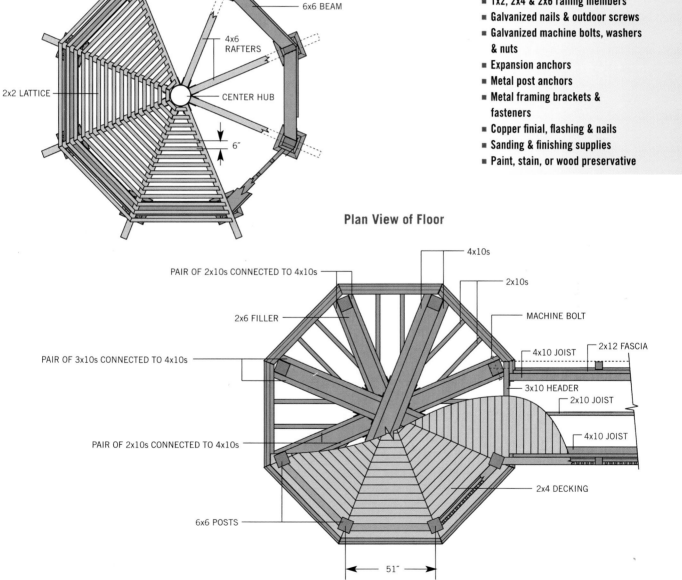

Plan View of Roof

6x6 BEAM

4x6 RAFTERS

2x2 LATTICE

CENTER HUB

6"

Plan View of Floor

4x10s

PAIR OF 2x10s CONNECTED TO 4x10s

2x10s

2x6 FILLER

MACHINE BOLT

PAIR OF 3x10s CONNECTED TO 4x10s

4x10 JOIST

2x12 FASCIA

3x10 HEADER

2x10 JOIST

PAIR OF 2x10s CONNECTED TO 4x10s

4x10 JOIST

2x4 DECKING

6x6 POSTS

51"

DINING OCTAGON

Mirroring the contours of an eight-sided brick patio, this elegant octagonal
pavilion creates a formal outdoor dining space adjacent to a built-in barbecue.
Subtle detailing, such as beveled moldings, chamfered posts, and a wrap-
around 1-by-6 frieze board, lends the structure an air of sophistication.
Landscape architect: Forsum/Summers & Partners.

DESIGN DETAILS

This structure isn't actually a true octagon but is slightly elongated, measuring about 18 feet wide by 21 feet long. Eight 6-by-6 redwood posts support a roof frame made of massive 4-by-12 Douglas fir beams, which in turn support a grid of 4 by 10s and a ceiling of lattice panels.

Each post is trimmed at top and bottom with mitered moldings reminiscent of the caps and bases found on classical columns.

An opaque white stain (brushed on after the parts were cut to size but before they were assembled) was applied to complement the home and give the pavilion a lighter, more contemporary look.

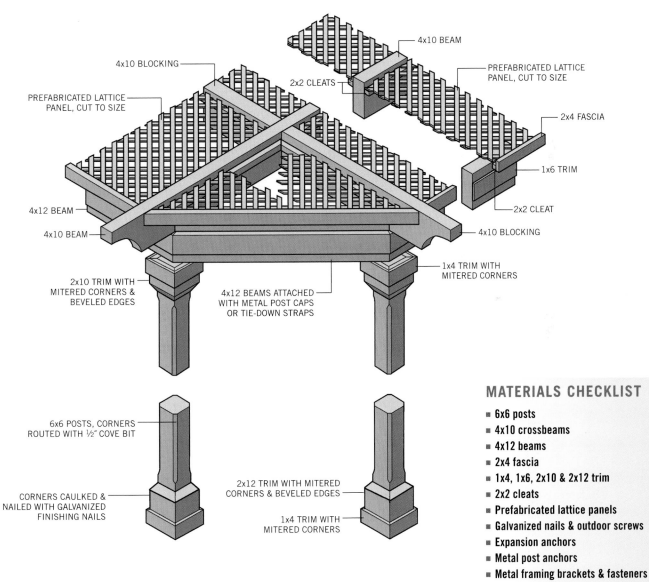

4x10 BEAM

4x10 BLOCKING

PREFABRICATED LATTICE PANEL, CUT TO SIZE

2x2 CLEATS

PREFABRICATED LATTICE PANEL, CUT TO SIZE

2x4 FASCIA

1x6 TRIM

2x2 CLEAT

4x12 BEAM

4x10 BEAM

4x10 BLOCKING

1x4 TRIM WITH MITERED CORNERS

2x10 TRIM WITH MITERED CORNERS & BEVELED EDGES

4x12 BEAMS ATTACHED WITH METAL POST CAPS OR TIE-DOWN STRAPS

6x6 POSTS, CORNERS ROUTED WITH ½" COVE BIT

2x12 TRIM WITH MITERED CORNERS & BEVELED EDGES

CORNERS CAULKED & NAILED WITH GALVANIZED FINISHING NAILS

1x4 TRIM WITH MITERED CORNERS

MATERIALS CHECKLIST

- 6x6 posts
- 4x10 crossbeams
- 4x12 beams
- 2x4 fascia
- 1x4, 1x6, 2x10 & 2x12 trim
- 2x2 cleats
- Prefabricated lattice panels
- Galvanized nails & outdoor screws
- Expansion anchors
- Metal post anchors
- Metal framing brackets & fasteners
- Sanding & finishing supplies
- Paint, stain, or wood preservative

Elevation Section View

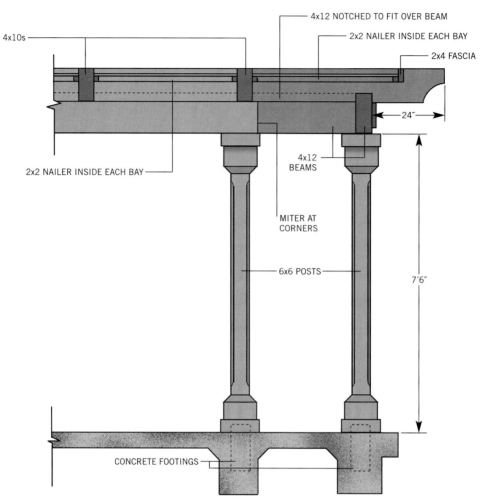

4x12 NOTCHED TO FIT OVER BEAM

4x10s

2x2 NAILER INSIDE EACH BAY

2x4 FASCIA

24"

2x2 NAILER INSIDE EACH BAY

4x12 BEAMS

MITER AT CORNERS

6x6 POSTS

7'6"

CONCRETE FOOTINGS

BUILDING NOTES

When attaching the posts to an existing masonry patio or wood deck, use metal post anchors. If you're building the pavilion over grass, dig and pour concrete footings for the posts, as described on pages 120–121. Metal connectors are also used to attach the beams to the tops of the posts and to strengthen the joints between the 4 by 10s.

The lattice panels are fastened to 2-by-2 nailers attached to the 4 by 10s that form the ceiling grid. Note that three 4 by 10s extend across the entire width of the structure. The 4 by 10s that run perpendicular are cut to fit in between the three long ones.

1 Mark the location of the eight posts. Fasten the post anchors to the patio by driving galvanized screws into lead expansion anchors. Cut each post to 7 feet, 6 inches long and chamfer the corners using a router and ½-inch cove bit. Stand the posts in the post anchors, brace them plumb with 1 by 4s, and secure them with galvanized screws.

2 Measure and cut the eight 4-by-12 beams that run from post to post. Miter-cut both ends of each beam, making sure that the miter joint falls at the center of each post. Fasten the beams to the tops of the posts with galvanized tie-down straps or post caps.

3 Next, cut the three long 4-by-10 beams that span the width of the structure. Each one should extend past the 4-by-12 perimeter beams by 24 inches. Cut the decorative radii at the ends of the beams with a reciprocating saw.

4 Set the 4 by 10s on top of the 4 by 12s, spacing them 5 feet, 6 inches on center. Mark each 4 by 10 where it intersects the 4 by 12s. Take down the 4 by 10s and cut a 2⅞-inch-deep-by-3½-inch-wide notch at each set of marks. Put the notched 4 by 10s on top of the perimeter beams and then secure them with 3-inch decking screws.

5 Now cut the shorter 4-by-10 cross-beams to fit between the long 4 by 10s. Space them 48 inches on center. Again, cut notches in the ones that cross the perimeter 4-by-12 beams. Use right-angle corner brackets to join the cross-beams to the long 4 by 10s.

6 With the ceiling frame completed, begin attaching the 2-by-2 nailers to the inside surfaces of the ceiling grid with their lower edges 3½ inches from the top edge of the 4 by 10s. Note that you also need to fasten 2 by 2s to the outside surfaces of the perimeter 4-by-12 beams. Then screw a 2-by-4 fascia to the perimeter 2-by-2 nailers.

7 Carefully measure and cut prefabricated lattice to fit into each square in the ceiling grid. Secure the lattice panels to the 2-by-2 nailers with 4d galvanized finishing nails. If the lattice splits when you nail it, bore pilot holes first with a ⅛-inch-diameter drill bit.

8 Cut the decorative frieze out of 1 by 6s. Attach the boards to the center of the 4-by-12 perimeter beams with 6d galvanized finishing nails.

9 Create the first layer of base molding around each post bottom by mitering pieces of 2 by 12. Bevel the tops of the pieces to 45 degrees, then nail them to the posts. Miter cut the 1-by-4 baseboard trim to fit around the 2-by-12 base, but don't bevel the top edges. Tack up the baseboard with 4d galvanized finishing nails.

10 Miter cut the 2-by-10 cap to fit around the top of each post. Bevel the bottom edge of the pieces to 45 degrees, then nail the pieces flush to the tops of the posts. Then miter cut the 1-by-4 trim to size. Nail the 1-by-4 pieces flush with the tops of the 2 by 10s with 4d galvanized finishing nails.

Plan View

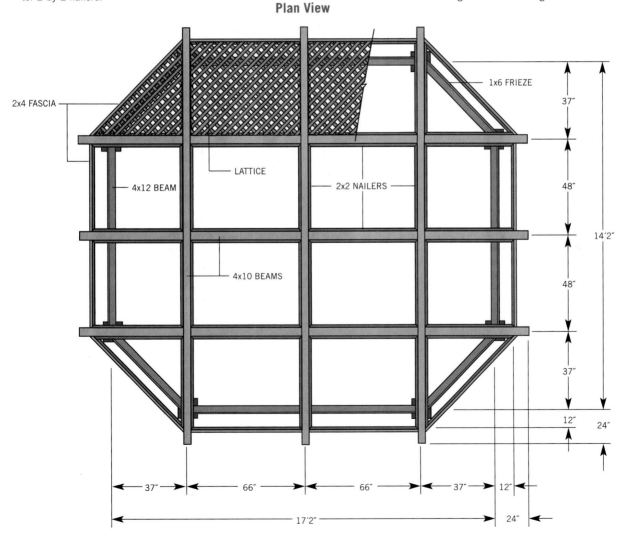

2x4 FASCIA

1x6 FRIEZE

LATTICE

4x12 BEAM

2x2 NAILERS

4x10 BEAMS

37″ 48″ 48″ 37″ 12″ 24″

14′2″

37″ 66″ 66″ 37″ 12″ 24″

17′2″

OPEN SHELTER

Conveniently located just a few steps from the house, this 10-by-14½-foot arbor invites family and friends outdoors to dine or otherwise enjoy the deck and garden space. The structure is located on the middle of three cascading decks that make the transition from the floor level of the house to the driveway and garden. Landscape architect: J. Starbuck.

DESIGN DETAILS

The use of three 6-by-6 posts at each corner defines the roomlike space, making railings unnecessary. If your structure is elevated or on a hillside, however, a railing made with a 2-by-6 top rail, 2-by-2 spindles on 4½-inch centers, and a 2-by-4 bottom rail can easily be attached on one or more sides. The area underneath can be framed with lattice for additional enclosure, to hide unwanted views, or simply to serve as a decorative element.

If, as in this case, your arbor serves as a passageway and dining area, make sure the dimensions of your dining table and chairs permit easy passage around them. This design also assures comfortable passage since the deck extends several feet past the arbor and has wide, low-rise stairs.

Trim details at the post tops and on the roof fascia add a distinctive touch.

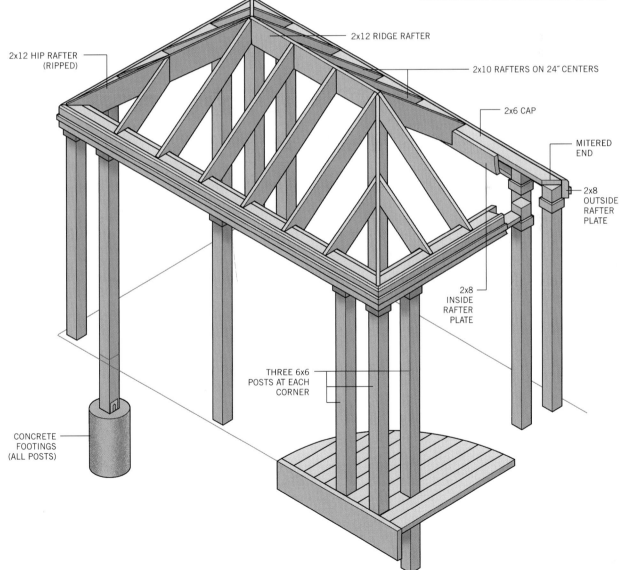

2x12 RIDGE RAFTER

2x12 HIP RAFTER (RIPPED)

2x10 RAFTERS ON 24" CENTERS

2x6 CAP

MITERED END

2x8 OUTSIDE RAFTER PLATE

2x8 INSIDE RAFTER PLATE

THREE 6x6 POSTS AT EACH CORNER

CONCRETE FOOTINGS (ALL POSTS)

BUILDING NOTES

This arbor can be built over a grade-level or elevated deck, or a patio. If the deck is being constructed at the same time, it may be able to share common posts/footings with the arbor.

Capping the posts with 2 by 6s not only holds the posts together but protects their end grain from absorbing excessive moisture.

Because the roof framing is exposed to view and the elements, appearance and tight joints are particularly important. This handsome design calls for a backed-up hip rafter or ridge board ripped to width so that one edge is flush with the bottom of the rafters and the top edge is beveled to align with the top of the rafters. Since wind uplift is not a factor for this open arbor, use bolts, long screws, and/or long nails instead of less attractive framing hardware, even though doing so is more labor-intensive. See Tools and Techniques, beginning on page 102, for complete information on tools and building procedures.

1 Form and pour the footings (see pages 120–121) so they extend down at least 12 inches or to your area's frost line. Embed post anchors in each footing to accept the columns. To prevent excessive moisture absorption through the end grain, make sure the posts do not sit directly on the concrete.

2 Cut the 6-by-6 posts to length and secure them to the post bases with bolts. Nail 2-by-6 caps, mitered at the outside corners, across the post tops. Brace all posts diagonally in both directions to hold them plumb.

3 For the two narrow "sides" of the structure, cut 2-by-8 inside rafter plates to lengths equal to the outside dimension of the posts' spans. Clamp them to the inner faces of the tops, flush with the 2-by-6 post caps, while you drill countersink and clearance holes. Fasten the inside rafter plates to the posts with bolts, washers, and nuts (or lag bolts).

4 For the long sides, cut the inside rafter plates to fit between the installed rafter plates and join them by end nailing. Clamp the rafter plates to the posts that are at mid span, double-check that the posts are plumb, and then drill for and install bolts as before.

Elevation View

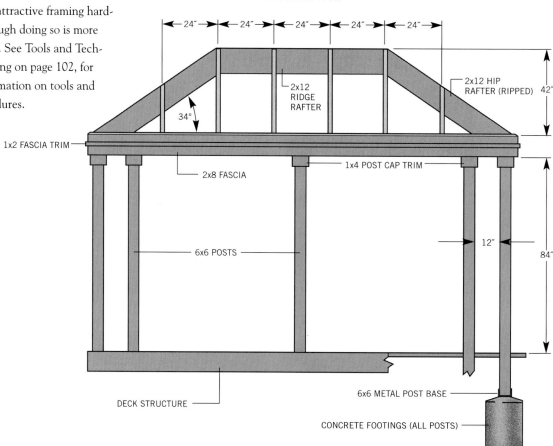

Plan View

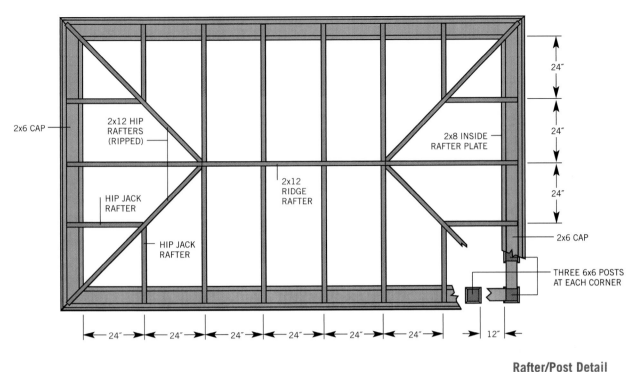

2x6 CAP

2x12 HIP RAFTERS (RIPPED)

HIP JACK RAFTER

HIP JACK RAFTER

2x12 RIDGE RAFTER

2x8 INSIDE RAFTER PLATE

24″

24″

24″

2x6 CAP

THREE 6x6 POSTS AT EACH CORNER

← 24″ → ← 24″ → ← 24″ → ← 24″ → ← 24″ → ← 24″ → → 12″ ←

5 Cut the angles on the top and bottom of the six common rafters so they fit flush with the outsides of the posts and against the 2-by-12 ridge rafter. Then cut the bird's-mouth notches so that each rafter fits over the 2-by-8 inside rafter plate as shown in the illustration at right.

6 Brace the ridge board in place while you attach the rafters to it and the 2-by-8 fascia. Next, cut, notch, and install the two common rafters at the center of each hip roof and attach them to the end of the ridge board and the rafter plate.

7 Using a framing square, determine the length and cutting angles for the 2-by-12 hip rafters. Cut and install the four hip rafters, which require double side cuts at both top and bottom. Make the cuts that form the bird's-mouth.

8 Next, cut, notch, and install the hip jack rafters. The top angle must have a single side cut where it meets the hip rafter. The theoretical length of these rafters must be shortened by half the 45-degree thickness of the hip rafter (which is about $1\frac{1}{16}$ inches).

9 Rip the bevel along the top edge of the 2-by-8 fascia boards. Cut them to length, miter the corners, and nail them to the ends of all the rafters and to the corner posts. Install the 1-by-2 fascia trim and 1-by-4 post cap trim with exterior adhesive and 8d galvanized nails (miter at corners).

10 Perform any final sanding that may be required. Apply an exterior stain suitable for the type of wood you have chosen to enhance its appearance and protect it from the elements.

Rafter/Post Detail

RAFTER

2x6 CAP

1x2 FASCIA TRIM

2x8 FASCIA

NOTCH RAFTER

2x8 INSIDE RAFTER PLATE

1x4 POST CAP TRIM

MATERIALS CHECKLIST

- Concrete, #4 rebar & form lumber for footings
- 6x6 posts
- 2x6 post caps
- 2x8 rafter plates & fascia
- 2x10 & 2x12 rafters
- 1x2 trim
- Galvanized nails & outdoor screws
- Galvanized machine bolts, washers & nuts
- Metal post anchors
- Metal framing brackets & fasteners
- Sanding & finishing supplies
- Paint, stain, or wood preservative

GARDEN PORTAL

A pair of 28-inch-long benches flank the 36-inch-wide passageway through this garden bower. The pastel-painted structure provides a place for peaceful contemplation, private conversation, or a relaxing break from work in the garden. Design: Elizabeth Lair.

DESIGN DETAILS

The designer's choice of 1-by lumber (mostly 1 by 2s) for this structure, rather than a mix of 1-by and 2-by lumber, simplifies construction and keeps materials costs down, yet it is quite sturdy for sitting.

The design is easily adapted for wider paths, and you can certainly experiment with different profiles for the arch that supports the roof trellis. Take extra care finishing the wood. Applying a wood preservative—and especially soaking the end grain—prior to priming and painting exterior wood surfaces helps prevent peeling and cracking that leads to total paint failure and rot.

BUILDING NOTES

The completed structure is lightweight, so you can build subassemblies or even the entire piece off site. Precut all parts for efficiency, to reduce the risk of error, and so you can apply a wood preservative, prefinish, and paint all pieces prior to assembly.

To make sure that the left and right sides of the arch, which must be drawn freehand, are mirror images, create a ¼-inch plywood template for one half, trace it onto your stock, then flip it over to mark the other half. Use this arch as a template for the second one.

Before cutting the strips for the diamonds, cut a couple and verify that they work in all locations. To prevent splitting the wood, bore pilot holes wherever screws are within 2 inches of the end of a board.

See Tools and Techniques, beginning on page 102, for complete information on tools and building procedures.

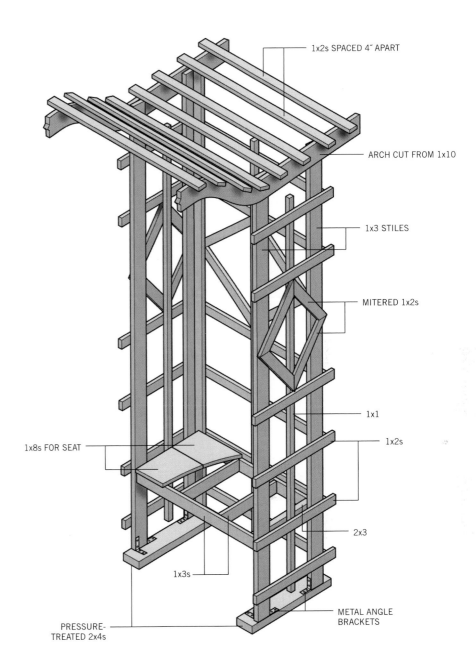

1x2s SPACED 4″ APART

ARCH CUT FROM 1x10

1x3 STILES

MITERED 1x2s

1x1

1x2s

2x3

1x8s FOR SEAT

1x3s

METAL ANGLE BRACKETS

PRESSURE-TREATED 2x4s

1 Cut all the parts, except the 1 by 2s for the diamonds. Cut the 1 by 2s: twenty at 18 inches, twelve at 29 inches, four at 12 inches, and fifteen at 35 inches. Finally, cut the 1-by-10 stock for the arch to two 83-inch lengths.

2 Draw and cut one arch with a jigsaw, then use it as a template to cut the other one. The 4-inch-wide arch rises to 4 inches in the center and rises 1 inch at each end. It is helpful to draw vertical lines where the curves begin or change direction—at the center point and above each inside stile.

Elevation View

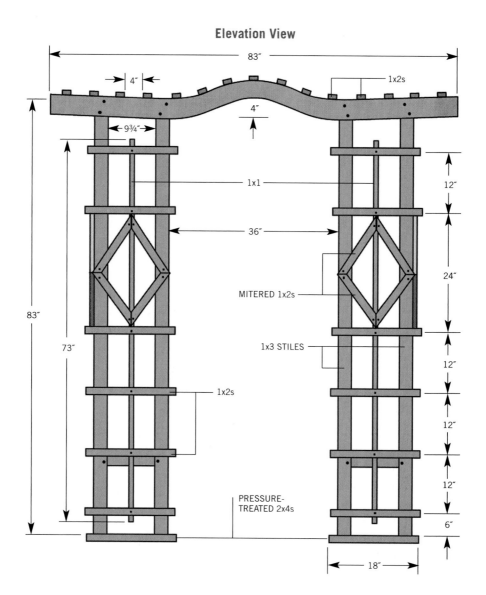

83″

4″

1x2s

9¾″

4″

12″

1x1

36″

24″

MITERED 1x2s

1x3 STILES

83″

73″

12″

1x2s

12″

12″

PRESSURE-
TREATED 2x4s

6″

18″

3 Soak the ends of all the pieces in a wood preservative that accepts paint. When the wood is completely dry, apply exterior primer to all surfaces, then a coat of paint. Apply a touch-up or final coat after assembly.

4 Make four identical ladder trellises as shown in the illustration on the facing page. Use 1¼-inch exterior screws through the 83-inch verticals into the backs of the 18-inch horizontals and use nails through the horizontals into the 73-inch center braces.

5 To determine the cuts for the pieces that form the diamonds, mark the vertical center on the rungs and the horizontal center between the rungs on the stiles. Then, hold a length of 1 by 2 in position and mark the angles. Secure with nails after preserving, priming, and painting.

6 Lay a pair of trellises flat on their outside faces, parallel to each other, 36 inches apart and with their ends aligned against a straightedge. Place an arch into position, centered under the trellis stiles, and secure it with two screws at each stile. Repeat for the other pair of trellises.

7 Next, secure the 83-inch 1-by-3 stiles to the trellis assemblies with nails placed every 8 inches. Assemble the support framework for each bench by nailing the 12-inch rungs, on edge, between the 29-inch rails.

8 Join two trellises with the five horizontal braces attached to the stiles using nails. Then attach the seat framework between them 18 inches up from the base with 2½-inch screws driven through the faces of the trellises into the ends of the framework. Repeat the procedure with the other two trellises.

Side Elevation View

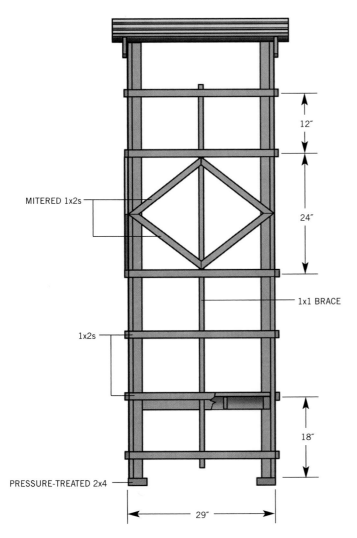

MITERED 1x2s

12″

24″

1x1 BRACE

1x2s

18″

PRESSURE-TREATED 2x4

29″

Plan View of Seat

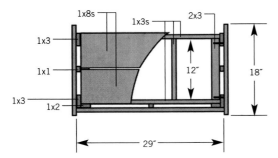

1x8s

1x3s

2x3

1x3

1x1

1x3

1x2

12″

18″

29″

9 Lay the assemblies on their sides, elevated a few inches to allow for the 2-inch overhang, and secure the top trellis members onto the arch supports with nails. Start at the center and work outward, using a wood block to assure uniform, 4-inch spacing.

10 Attach pressure-treated 2-by-4 feet onto the legs with metal angle brackets. Level the ground and stand the trellis up to install the back center support and the benches on either side. Attach the feet to stakes driven into the ground. Cut the stakes off flush with the top of the feet.

MATERIALS CHECKLIST

- 2x4 pressure-treated sills
- 1x2 trellis stock
- 1x3s
- 1x10s
- 2x3s
- ¼-inch plywood (for template)
- Galvanized nails & outdoor screws
- Metal angle brackets & screws
- Wood stakes
- Sanding & finishing supplies
- Paint, stain, or wood preservative

BI-LEVEL SHADE STRUCTURE

Six round posts stand like trees to support this two-tiered shade structure. The 6-inch-diameter treated lodge poles, purchased from a landscape supplier, are through-bolted to a canopy of crisscrossing Douglas fir 2-by beams and shade-producing 3 by 3s. Before assembly, all of the lumber was lightly sandblasted, then stained white to create an attractive sun-bleached appearance. Landscape architect: Forsum/Summers & Partners.

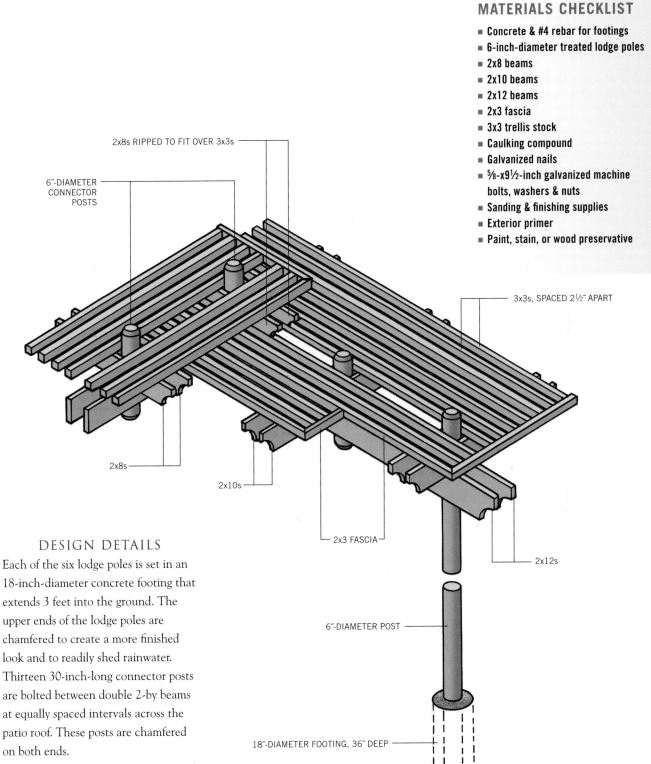

2x8s RIPPED TO FIT OVER 3x3s

6˝-DIAMETER CONNECTOR POSTS

3x3s, SPACED 2½˝ APART

2x8s

2x10s

2x3 FASCIA

2x12s

6˝-DIAMETER POST

18˝-DIAMETER FOOTING, 36˝ DEEP

MATERIALS CHECKLIST

- Concrete & #4 rebar for footings
- 6-inch-diameter treated lodge poles
- 2x8 beams
- 2x10 beams
- 2x12 beams
- 2x3 fascia
- 3x3 trellis stock
- Caulking compound
- Galvanized nails
- ⅝-x9½-inch galvanized machine bolts, washers & nuts
- Sanding & finishing supplies
- Exterior primer
- Paint, stain, or wood preservative

DESIGN DETAILS

Each of the six lodge poles is set in an 18-inch-diameter concrete footing that extends 3 feet into the ground. The upper ends of the lodge poles are chamfered to create a more finished look and to readily shed rainwater. Thirteen 30-inch-long connector posts are bolted between double 2-by beams at equally spaced intervals across the patio roof. These posts are chamfered on both ends.

On top of the beams is a two-tiered lattice canopy constructed of 3 by 3s framed by 2-by-3 fascia boards. Lumberyards don't typically stock 3 by 3s, but they can be special ordered.

Bi-level Shade Structure **63**

BUILDING NOTES

Before ordering the lumber, measure out and mark the locations of the six posts, as shown in the plan view drawing opposite. Be careful not to position any of the posts close to a tree, large shrub, fence, or other stationary object because you'll need ample room to set up a ladder and maneuver the long beams into place.

Depending on the nature of the soil, you may be able to dig the footing holes with a shovel and post-hole digger. If the soil is very hard or rocky, however, rent a power auger or hire a landscaper who has an auger attachment on a back hoe.

See Tools and Techniques, beginning on page 102, for complete information on tools and building procedures.

1 Cut the six lodge poles to length and chamfer one end of each pole using a circular saw or handsaw and belt sander. Cut the 13 connector posts to 30 inches long and chamfer both ends of each one. Also cut to length all the 2-by beams, then cut the decorative 7¼-inch radius from the ends of each beam with a saber saw.

2 Locate and dig the six footing holes. Line the bottom of each hole with 2 inches of gravel to form a solid base and promote good drainage. Stand the round posts into the holes and hold them plumb with temporary 1-by-4 braces and stakes. Mix up about five 60-pound bags of concrete for each hole. Pour the concrete around each post up to grade, then smooth it with a trowel so it slopes slightly

away from the post. Allow the concrete to cure overnight. Be sure to seal the joints between the posts and concrete with caulking compound.

3 With a helper on another ladder, hold a 2-by-12 beam 7 feet above the ground against the two posts in the center of the structure. Position the beam so it extends out the same distance from each post, check it for level, then mark the post where it will attach to the beam.

4 Take down the 2 by 12 and lay it on top of another 2 by 12. Bore two ⅝-inch-diameter bolt holes through each beam at each mark. Repeat this procedure for the second set of 2 by 12 beams along the outer edge of the structure.

Elevation View

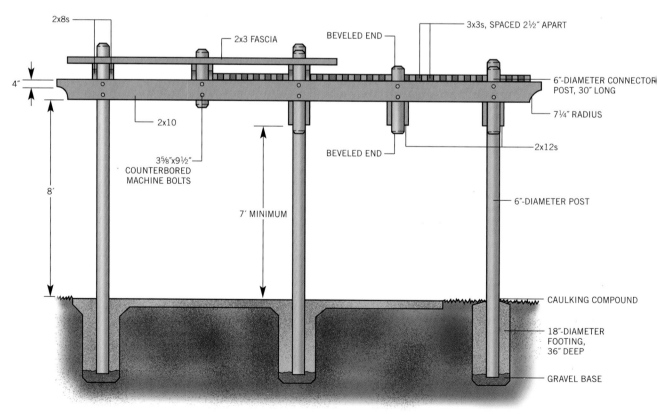

2x8s

2x3 FASCIA

BEVELED END

3x3s, SPACED 2½" APART

4"

6"-DIAMETER CONNECTOR POST, 30" LONG

2x10

7¼" RADIUS

3⅝"x9½" COUNTERBORED MACHINE BOLTS

BEVELED END

2x12s

8'

6"-DIAMETER POST

7' MINIMUM

CAULKING COMPOUND

18"-DIAMETER FOOTING, 36" DEEP

GRAVEL BASE

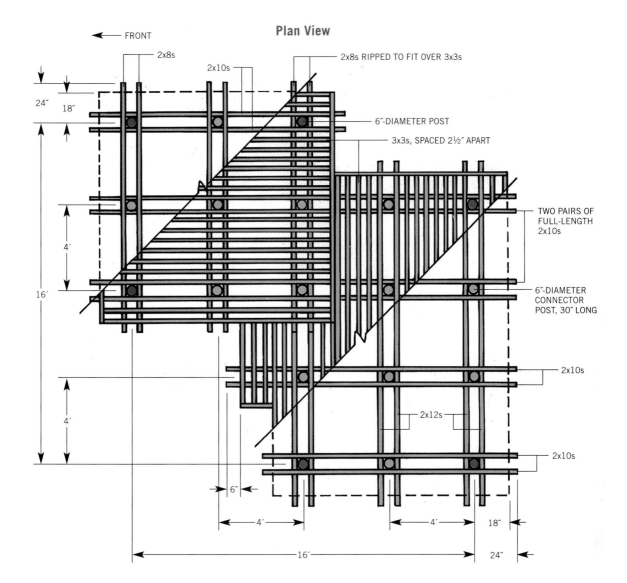

Plan View

← FRONT

2x8s

2x10s

2x8s RIPPED TO FIT OVER 3x3s

6″-DIAMETER POST

3x3s, SPACED 2½″ APART

TWO PAIRS OF FULL-LENGTH 2x10s

6″-DIAMETER CONNECTOR POST, 30″ LONG

2x10s

2x12s

2x10s

24″ 18″

16′

4′

4′

6″

4′

4′ 18″

16′ 24″

5 Lift the first 2 by 12 back into position, check for level, then bore into the bolt holes and through the posts with a ⅝-inch-diameter spade bit with an extension. Insert ⅝-inch-diameter-by-9½-inch-long galvanized carriage or machine bolts into the holes in the beam and posts. Slide the second beam onto the bolts on the other side of the post, slip on washers, and tighten on nuts. Install the pair of 2-by-12 beams along the outer edge of the structure in the same manner.

6 Bolt on the five pairs of 2-by-10 cross-beams that sit on top of the 2 by 12s. (Note from the illustration above that two of the 2-by-10 beams extend the full width of the patio roof.) Next, install the three pairs of 2-by-8 beams across the top of the three back 2 by 10s. Attach them with 9½-inch-long galvanized carriage or machine bolts.

7 Install all the connector posts into the square spaces created by the intersecting beams—seven on the lower tier, four on the upper tier, and two that pass through both tiers. Attach them with carriage or machine bolts.

8 Hang the last pair of 2-by-12 beams from the connecting posts bolted to the 2 by 10s at the midway point of the lower tier. As usual, use two bolts at each post.

9 Create the trellis by nailing 3 by 3s across the top of both tiers. Space them 2½ inches apart and fasten them to the beams with 20d galvanized nails.

10 Cut a fascia out of 2 by 3s to fit around each of the trellises. Miter the ends of the boards to create a finished frame. Attach the fascia by nailing into the ends of the 3 by 3s and by toenailing down into the beams with 16d galvanized nails.

Bi-level Shade Structure **65**

OPEN-AIR GAZEBO

A backyard sun deck offers a peaceful, private place to enjoy fresh air and sunshine. But even the most ardent sun worshiper needs a little shade every now and then. In addition to providing a cool, shady spot to sit and relax, even in the midday sun, this open-air gazebo serves as the focal point of the deck. Design: Jean-Claude Hurni, Architect.

DESIGN DETAILS

This gazebo measures just 8 by 8 feet at its base so it's an easy fit for even the most modest-sized deck or patio. Four 4-by-4 posts support a hip roof comprised primarily of 2 by 6s with a perimeter beam of double 2 by 8s. Along the lower edge of the roof is a series of cantilevered rafter tails with a decorative ogee profile. Three 2-by-2 lattice strips are fastened to the tops of the rafter tails to create a distinctive shadow pattern around the perimeter—and they're also handy for hanging a variety of potted plants.

Each of the four support posts and the short 4 by 4 at the roof peak is topped with a decorative wood finial.

Casting just enough shade to keep the deck dappled in soft sunlight and shadows, this gazebo's open, airy structure is inviting and not at all imposing.

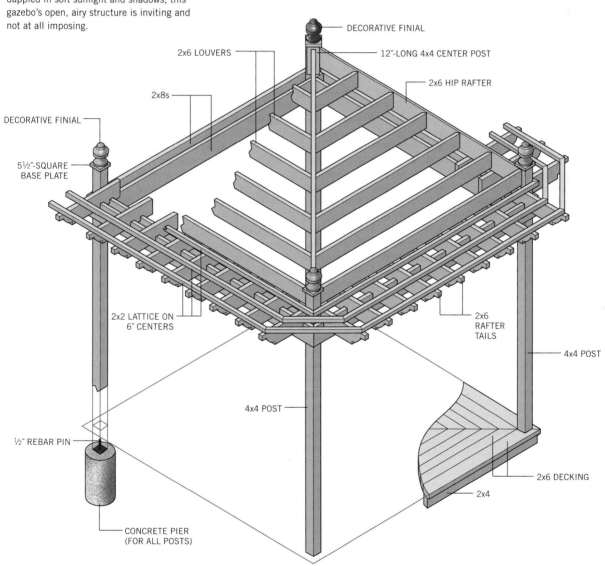

DECORATIVE FINIAL

2x6 LOUVERS

12"-LONG 4x4 CENTER POST

2x8s

2x6 HIP RAFTER

DECORATIVE FINIAL

5½"-SQUARE BASE PLATE

2x2 LATTICE ON 6" CENTERS

2x6 RAFTER TAILS

4x4 POST

4x4 POST

½" REBAR PIN

2x6 DECKING

2x4

CONCRETE PIER (FOR ALL POSTS)

BUILDING NOTES

Each of the four 4-by-4 posts passes through the decking and sits on top of a concrete pier. The pier holes must be dug down to the frost line or a minimum of 18 inches.

The posts are attached to the concrete piers with rebar pins. The pins are inserted into each pier, the bottom of each post is bored with a hole, then once the concrete has cured, the posts are slipped over the pins.

If you're adding the gazebo to an existing deck, check with local building codes. You might be allowed to attach the posts to the deck's floor joists with galvanized carriage bolts.

1 Pour the four concrete piers and insert ½-inch-diameter-by-12-inch-long metal reinforcing bars 8 inches down into the wet concrete. Then bore a ½-inch-diameter-by-4-inch-deep hole into the bottom of each post. Allow the concrete to cure for 24 hours.

2 Apply a thick, circular bead of exterior-grade caulk around the pins. Then cut four 4-by-4-inch gaskets out of an asphalt roof shingle. Punch a ½-inch-diameter hole in the center of the gaskets and slip them over the pins. Press the gaskets down against the concrete piers and apply another circular bead of caulk to the tops of the gaskets. Bore a ½-inch-diameter-by-4-inch-deep hole in the bottom of each post and slip the posts over the pins. Plumb each post with a 4-foot level to

ensure they're perfectly vertical, then attach the posts to a floor joist with long lag screws or carriage bolts.

3 Cut to length the eight 2-by-8 horizontal beams that run along the outside and inside of the posts. Fasten the beams to the posts with galvanized carriage bolts.

4 Cut the 21 rafter tails to 28 inches long from 2-by-6 stock. Using a saber saw, form the decorative ogee profile at one end of each piece.

Elevation Section View

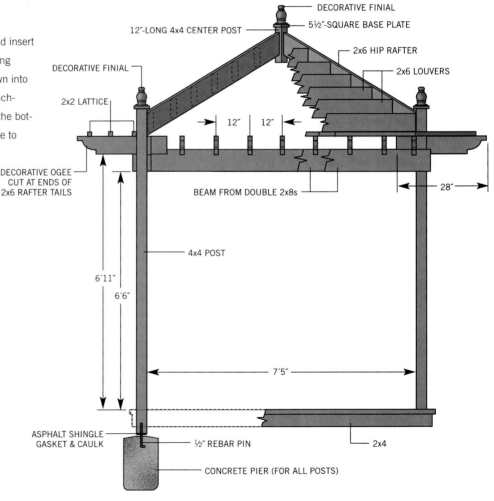

DECORATIVE FINIAL
5½"-SQUARE BASE PLATE
12"-LONG 4x4 CENTER POST
2x6 HIP RAFTER
2x6 LOUVERS
DECORATIVE FINIAL
2x2 LATTICE
12" 12"
DECORATIVE OGEE CUT AT ENDS OF 2x6 RAFTER TAILS
BEAM FROM DOUBLE 2x8s
28"
4x4 POST
6'11"
6'6"
7'5"
ASPHALT SHINGLE GASKET & CAULK
½" REBAR PIN
2x4
CONCRETE PIER (FOR ALL POSTS)

MATERIALS CHECKLIST

- Concrete & #4 rebar for footings
- 4x4 posts
- 2x8 beams
- 2x6 rafters & rafter tails
- 2x2 trellis stock
- Caulking compound
- Galvanized nails & outdoor screws
- Galvanized lag screws & washers
- Metal post anchors or rebar pins
- Sanding & finishing supplies
- Exterior primer
- Paint, stain, or wood preservative

Plan View

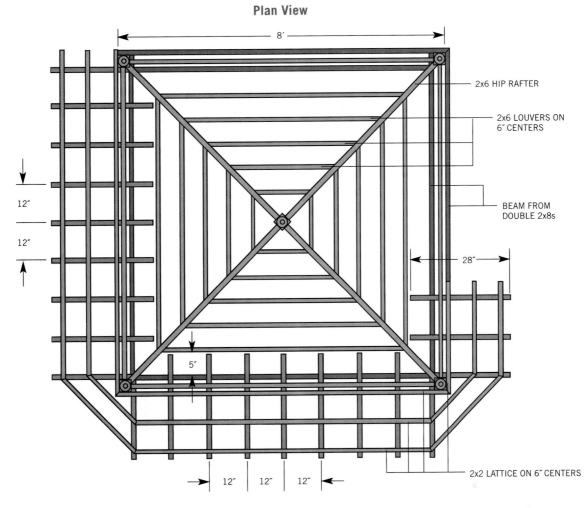

2x6 HIP RAFTER

2x6 LOUVERS ON 6″ CENTERS

BEAM FROM DOUBLE 2x8s

8′

12″

12″

28″

5″

12″   12″   12″

2x2 LATTICE ON 6″ CENTERS

5 With a portable circular saw, cut the 1½-inch-deep-by-6½-inch-wide notches that allow the rafter tails to fit over the beams. Start each notch 5 inches from the square end of the rafter tails, which will leave 16½ inches of each tail cantilevered over the edge of the outer beams. Space the rafter tails 12 inches on center, bore pilot holes, and fasten to the beams with 2½-inch decking screws.

6 Cut the four hip rafters out of 2 by 6s and install with the aid of a helper. Each rafter runs from a corner post up to the peak of the 12-inch-long center post. Secure the rafters with 2½-inch decking screws driven into the corner posts and center post.

7 Next, install the series of tiered 2-by-6 louvers that start at the base of the roof, near the top of the four corner posts, and continue all the way up to the peak. Six 2-by-6 louvers, spaced 6 inches on center, are required for each of the four sides of the roof. Miter-cut the ends of the boards at 45 degrees, then screw the boards to the rafters.

8 Cut 2 by 2s to length to create the lattice strips for the tops of the rafter tails. Space the strips 6 inches on center and secure them with 3-inch decking screws. At the corners, where the 2 by 2s form a 45-degree angle, miter-cut the ends of the strips to 22½ degrees. Be sure each miter joint falls directly on a rafter tail.

9 Finish off the top of the four corner posts and the short post at the peak with a base plate and finial. Cut the 5½-inch-square base plates from a 1-by-6 board. Fasten them to the tops of the posts with exterior-grade caulk and 8d galvanized finishing nails. Bore a center hole for the finials' mounting screws, then screw the finials to the posts.

10 Paint or stain the gazebo, as desired. (You may want to do this before assembling the structure.) Use a semi-transparent stain to maintain the wood's natural color. If you choose not to apply a paint or stain, brush on a coat of clear wood preservative to protect the gazebo from the harmful effects of sun and moisture.

LATTICE PAVILION

A sturdy timber frame and airy lattice panels combine to lend a casual elegance to this poolside retreat. The 4-by-4 posts and 4-by-8 beams support an overhead covering of prefabricated lattice, which creates cool shadows and dappled sunlight. All of the parts were finished with an opaque stain before assembly to eliminate any chance of stain dripping onto the brick patio. Landscape architect: John J. Greenwood & Associates, Inc.

DESIGN DETAILS

The outer surfaces of the posts and beams are trimmed with 2 by 4s, which create shadow lines and add visual interest to the structure. Lattice extensions measuring 12 inches wide flank the posts and beams and give the pavilion a substantial look.

The ceiling is made up of crisscrossing 4-by-8 beams that form a grid of 3-foot, 3-inch squares. The lattice panel in each square is sandwiched between 2-by-2 cleats nailed to the sides of the beams. When the pavilion is viewed from below, the effect is that of a coffered ceiling.

BUILDING NOTES

This poolside pavilion was built atop an existing brick patio, but it could also be erected over a wood deck, concrete patio, or level expanse of lawn. Note that the 4-by-4 posts are secured to the brick patio with metal post anchors. If you build the pavilion over a different surface, see pages 120–121 for the best method of setting the posts.

When laying out the locations of the five 4-by-4 posts, be sure that the distance between any two posts does not exceed 16 feet.

Cut and stain all of the timber parts before you assemble the frame, but do not cut and stain the lattice panels until after the frame has been erected so that you can cut each panel to precisely fit the ceiling grid.

See Tools and Techniques, beginning on page 102, for complete information on tools and building procedures.

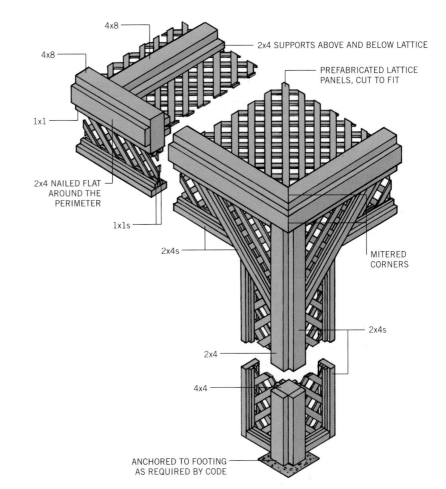

4x8

4x8

1x1

2x4 NAILED FLAT AROUND THE PERIMETER

1x1s

2x4s

2x4

4x4

ANCHORED TO FOOTING AS REQUIRED BY CODE

2x4 SUPPORTS ABOVE AND BELOW LATTICE

PREFABRICATED LATTICE PANELS, CUT TO FIT

MITERED CORNERS

2x4s

1 Measure out the locations of the post anchors and mark the screw-mounting holes onto the patio surface. Drill the holes with a masonry bit, then tap in expansion anchors. Fasten the anchors with galvanized lag screws.

2 Cut the five 4-by-4 posts to 8 feet long and hold each post upright with temporary 1-by-4 braces. Check for plumb, then secure the posts to the post anchors with weather-resistant galvanized or stainless-steel screws.

3 Measure from post to post and cut 4-by-8 beams to form the perimeter of the structure. Set the beams atop the posts and secure them by driving screws at an angle through the posts. Then screw a 4-inch metal angle bracket to the inside of each corner joint where one beam meets another at a right angle.

4 After installing the beams around the perimeter of the structure, cut the 4-by-8 beams that span the width of the ceiling. Space the beams 42½ inches on center and secure them to the perimeter beams with metal angle brackets.

Plan View of Framework

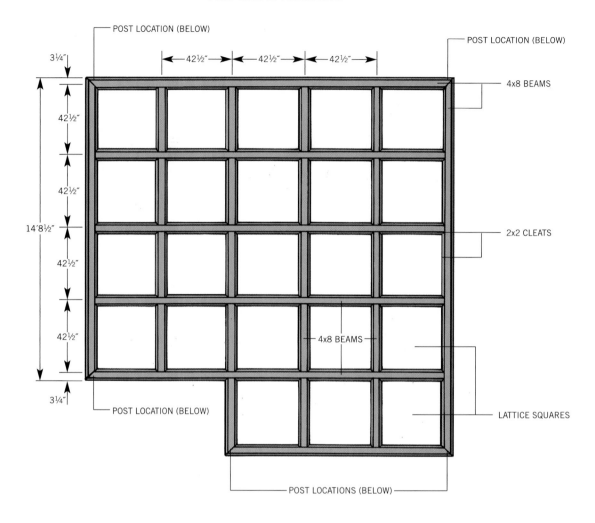

POST LOCATION (BELOW)

3¼"

42½" 42½" 42½"

42½"

42½"

14'8½"

42½"

42½"

3¼"

POST LOCATION (BELOW)

POST LOCATION (BELOW)

POST LOCATION (BELOW)

4x8 BEAMS

2x2 CLEATS

4x8 BEAMS

LATTICE SQUARES

POST LOCATIONS (BELOW)

5 Measure and cut the crossbeams to fit between the long ceiling beams. Space them 3 feet, 6½ inches on center and attach them with metal brackets.

6 Next, install 2-by-4 diagonal bracing at each corner. Screw a 10½-inch-long treated 2-by-4 sill to the patio beside each post. Nail up the vertical 2 by 4s that go from the sill to the diagonal bracing. Then attach the horizontal 2 by 4s that span from one diagonal brace to the other.

7 Cut the 2-by-4 trim pieces for the 4-by-4 posts and 4-by-8 perimeter beams. Attach them with 10d galvanized finishing nails.

8 Measure down 2 inches from the tops of the beams that form the ceiling grid and attach 2-by-2 cleats so that the top edge of the cleats is on the 2-inch line. Cut lattice to fit each grid square, then secure the lattice with a second set of 2-by-2 cleats nailed to the beams.

9 Cut the lattice panels to fit into the 2-by-4 frames that extend from the side of each post and below the beams around the perimeter of the pavilion.

10 Secure the lattice extensions to the 2-by-4 sills and frames with 1-by-1 cleats. Rip these narrow pieces from 1-by lumber and fasten them with 4d galvanized finishing nails.

Roof Elevation Detail

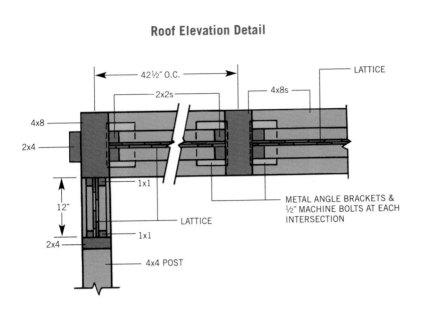

42½" O.C.

2x2s

LATTICE

4x8s

4x8

2x4

1x1

12"

LATTICE

1x1

2x4

METAL ANGLE BRACKETS &
½" MACHINE BOLTS AT EACH
INTERSECTION

4x4 POST

MATERIALS CHECKLIST

- 2x4 pressure-treated sills
- 4x4 posts
- 4x8 beams
- 2x4 framing
- Prefabricated lattice panels
- 2x4 stringers
- 2x4 trim
- 1x1 cleats
- 2x2 cleats
- Galvanized nails
- Galvanized lag screws & washers
- Expansion anchors
- Metal post anchors
- Galvanized metal angle brackets &
  ½-inch machine bolts
- Sanding & finishing supplies
- Paint, stain, or wood preservative

Elevation Section View

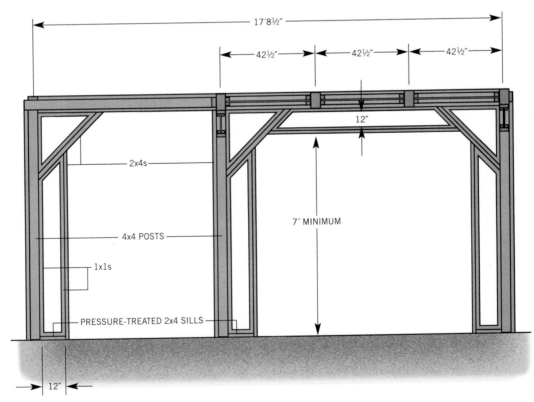

17'8½"

42½"   42½"   42½"

12"

2x4s

7' MINIMUM

4x4 POSTS

1x1s

PRESSURE-TREATED 2x4 SILLS

12"

Lattice Pavilion **73**

ARBOR BENCH

This handsome free-standing 5-foot-long arbor bench can add a touch of romance to any garden. Trellis beams, backrest, seat, and lattice side panels give the structure stability. The perfect nook for one or two, it's a private, sheltered place shaded by vines and scented by flowers. Designer/builder: Peter O. Whitely.

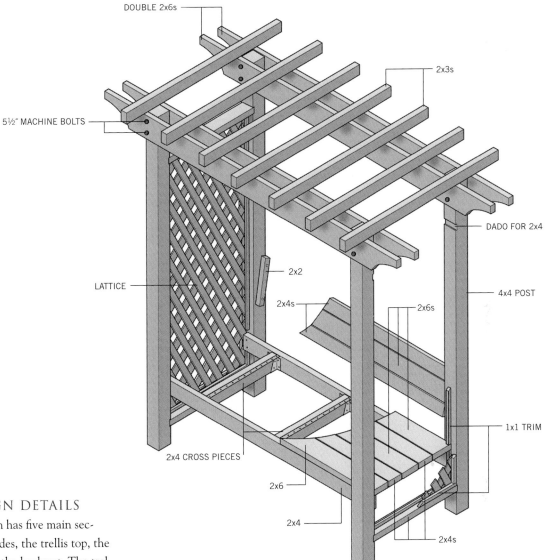

DOUBLE 2x6s

2x3s

5½" MACHINE BOLTS

DADO FOR 2x4

LATTICE

2x2

4x4 POST

2x4s

2x6s

1x1 TRIM

2x4 CROSS PIECES

2x6

2x4

2x4s

DESIGN DETAILS

The arbor bench has five main sections: the two sides, the trellis top, the bench seat, and the backrest. The trellis top, which consists of two pairs of horizontal 2 by 6s and seven 2-by-3 cross pieces, is added piece by piece.

The structure has a number of subtle features that add to its appearance, strength, and comfort. It is designed so that no nails or screws show, and copper-pipe end caps mask countersunk carriage bolts. A deep seat and angled backrest make the structure sturdy while providing comfort. The lattice side panels and overhead trellis are fashioned to train and support vines.

BUILDING NOTES

Anyone with average woodworking skills can build this project in a weekend. It can be assembled in a garage or workshop, then carried (with a few able helpers) to its final destination. Or it can be built as a unit, broken down into four main sections, and reassembled on site.

The structure is broad and stable enough to stand on its own, but for a more permanent installation, it can be anchored to concrete footings with metal brackets embedded in them.

This bench was built with standard-dimension select-heart redwood, but cedar, fir, or pressure-treated lumber will work just as well. If the intention is to paint the structure, plastic lattice could be used instead of wood.

MATERIALS CHECKLIST

- 4x4 posts
- 2x4 framing
- 2x6s
- 2x2 backer boards
- Prefabricated lattice panels
- Galvanized nails & outdoor screws
- ⅜-x5½-inch galvanized machine bolts, washers & nuts
- Undermount deck fastening brackets
- 2x4 joist hangers & nails
- 1-inch copper pipe end caps
- Sanding & finishing supplies
- Paint, stain, or wood preservative

Front Elevation View

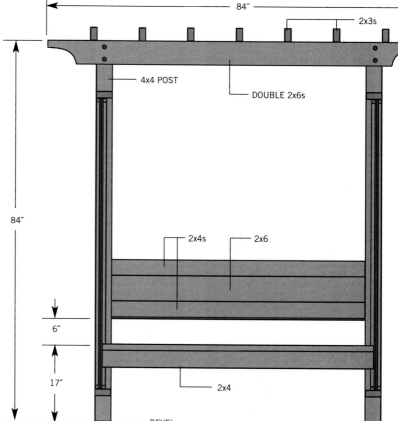

1 Cut the 4-by-4 posts 84 inches long and bevel the bottom edges of each one to prevent splintering. Measuring from the bottom end of each post, mark points at 6 and 7½, 70½ and 72 inches. Set the blade of a circular saw to extend ¼ inch, then remove the wood between the pairs of lines (make ¼-inch dado cuts).

2 Cut four 2-by-4 cross pieces the width of the lattice panels (typically 24 inches) plus ½ inch. Turn pairs of posts so they face each other, place the cross pieces in the grooves, and secure with two angled 3½-inch deck screws. Cut the lattice panels to length, about 63 inches.

3 Cut 1 by 1s to fit between the posts and nail them to the cross pieces flush to their outside edges. Cut and nail 1 by 1s to fit vertically between the cross pieces. Insert the lattice panels, then hold in place with 1 by 1s at top and bottom. Mark a point 17 inches from the bottom of each post, measure, cut, and nail lengths of 1 by 1 to extend from the top cross piece down to this point. (After the seat is in place, cut and nail 1 by 1 to fit between the seat and bottom cross piece.)

4 To create the bench frame, equally space three 2-by-4 cross pieces between two 5-foot-long 2 by 4s and secure with joist hangers and nails. Add undermount deck fastening brackets to the top of each cross piece.

5 Cut one 10-foot-long 2 by 4 and two 10-foot 2 by 6s into 5-foot lengths. Alternate three of the 2 by 6s with the two 2 by 4s. Position the frame on top so the outer 2 by 6s are flush with its edge, equally space the middle boards, and attach with outdoor screws.

6 Stand the side panels on their back edges and slip in the bench so its top butts against the 1 by 1s on the inside faces of the posts, then drive two 3½-inch screws through the bench frame and into each post.

7 Measure the distance between the two back posts and cut two 2 by 4s and one 2 by 6 to this size. Space the boards ⅛ inch apart, rip a 2 by 4, then overlay and attach the 12-inch 2 by 2s, flush to the ends, with 2½-inch screws. Slip the back in place so the bottom board is 6 inches above the seat and the 2-by-2 backer boards are centered on the posts. Angle the back to a comfortable position, then drive two screws through each of the backer boards.

8 Cut four 7-foot-long 2 by 6s and cut the ogees at the ends of each beam with a saber saw. Clamp a pair of beams to the front and back of the front posts so they're flush with the tops and extend equally on each side. Using a square as a guide, drill perfectly perpendicular holes with a ¹⁵⁄₁₆-inch spade bit through the front 2 by 6, the post, and almost through the back 2 by 6. Push in machine bolts with washers and nuts. Repeat for the back set of posts.

9 Cut seven 48-inch-long 2 by 3s, ripped from 2 by 6s. Mark points, evenly spaced (approximately 9 inches apart) for the 2 by 3s. Position them so they extend equally front and back and secure with 3½-inch deck screws.

10 Sand all of the wood surfaces except for the lattice and, using a pump sprayer, apply clear sealer to all. When dry, apply a second coat. When that is dry, insert the copper-pipe end caps in the holes for the countersunk bolts. Hammer or glue into position.

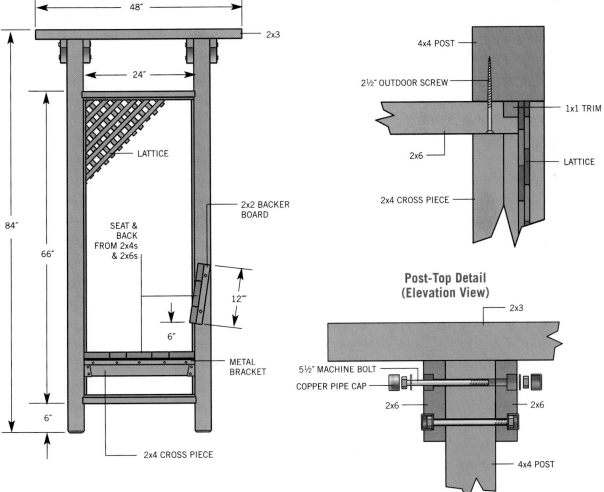

Side Elevation View

48″

2x3

24″

LATTICE

2x2 BACKER BOARD

84″

66″

SEAT & BACK FROM 2x4s & 2x6s

12″

6″

METAL BRACKET

6″

2x4 CROSS PIECE

Seat Support Detail (Plan Section View)

4x4 POST

2½″ OUTDOOR SCREW

1x1 TRIM

2x6

LATTICE

2x4 CROSS PIECE

Post-Top Detail (Elevation View)

2x3

5½″ MACHINE BOLT

COPPER PIPE CAP

2x6

2x6

4x4 POST

CONTEMPORARY TRELLIS

This 13-foot-wide by 12-foot-long shade trellis extends over multilevel decks, shedding filtered light on them and into the house through the sliding doors. It is painted white to match the home's trim and the deck railings. Designer/builder: Henry Angeli.

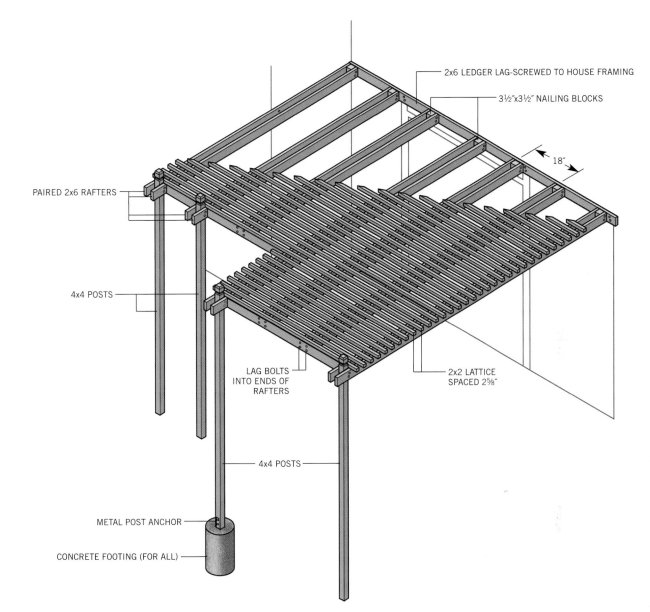

PAIRED 2x6 RAFTERS

4x4 POSTS

2x6 LEDGER LAG-SCREWED TO HOUSE FRAMING

3½″x3½″ NAILING BLOCKS

18″

LAG BOLTS
INTO ENDS OF
RAFTERS

2x2 LATTICE
SPACED 2⅝″

4x4 POSTS

METAL POST ANCHOR

CONCRETE FOOTING (FOR ALL)

DESIGN DETAILS

While not structurally necessary, the paired-rafter detail adds interest to the design, as do the routed channel and chamfer details at the post tops. By specifying nailing blocks between the rafter pairs, the design enables very solid connections without the use of utilitarian joist hangers.

Painting the trellis to match the trim and deck railings integrates the structure with the home and deck. While this trellis is designed to extend over a second, grade-level deck and the yard, the easily adapted design could be stepped or angled to conform to the shape of any deck.

The choice of redwood, which accepts and holds a painted finish much better than pressure-treated lumber does, is ideal. To prevent stains from natural resins, which are especially noticeable when the tannin bleeds through white or light-colored paint, use an oil-based primer to seal the wood. Premium quality 100 percent acrylic-latex exterior paint is the best topcoat.

MATERIALS CHECKLIST

- Concrete & #4 rebar for footing
- 4x4 posts
- 2x4 rafters & fascia
- 2x6 rafters & ledger
- 2x2 trellis stock
- Galvanized nails & outdoor screws
- 5⁄16-x3-inch galvanized lag screws & washers
- 3⁄8-x5-inch galvanized carriage bolts, washers & nuts
- Metal post anchors
- Sanding & finishing supplies
- Wood preservative
- Exterior primer
- Acrylic-latex exterior paint

BUILDING NOTES

Although this trellis was designed and built by an accomplished furniture maker, the structure is very easy to construct. The use of post anchors made it easy to cut the posts precisely before they were installed. The 2 by 2s for the trellis were cut with a table saw from 2-by-4 stock to save on the high price of 2-by-2 redwood.

To guide the positioning of the 2 by 2s for a uniform overhang, rip a 2 by 4 to the overhang dimension and clamp it onto the outside of the end rafters. Then start installing the 2 by 2s at the outer edge and work toward the house. Make a couple of U-shape jigs to hang over the rafters and set the desired spacing. As you near the house, check the remaining space against the num-

ber of 2 by 2s left. Make minor adjustments in the spacing, as needed, to avoid having the last one fall either too close or too far from where you want it.

1 Locate the post positions by measuring and squaring off from the house. Dig holes that extend 6 inches below your area's frost line, or at least 12 inches deep, pour footings, and embed post anchors for 4 by 4s in concrete as described on pages 120–121.

2 Cut the ledger and attach nailing blocks with 5/16-by-3-inch lag screws. Then bolt the ledger to the house framing. Methods vary widely depending on a house's siding type and the location of the framing. Consult your local building department for specifications.

3 Position the posts on post anchors. Drill clearance holes for 3/8-by-5-inch carriage bolts. Using a spirit level with a long straightedge, or a water level, mark a point on each post that is level with the bottom of the ledger.

4 Remove the posts and cut their tops 9½ inches above the marks. Cut a ½-by-½-inch dado around the posts using a router or a circular saw and chisel. Chamfer the top ½ inch of each post at a 45-degree angle. Reinstall the posts and brace them plumb.

5 Cut the rafters that attach to the posts to length. Bore clearance holes through the rafters, and pilot holes into the post and nailing blocks at the ledger. Attach the rafters to the insides of the posts with 5/16-by-3-inch lag screws and washers and to the ledger with 5/16-by-3½-inch carriage bolts, washers, and nuts.

Elevation View

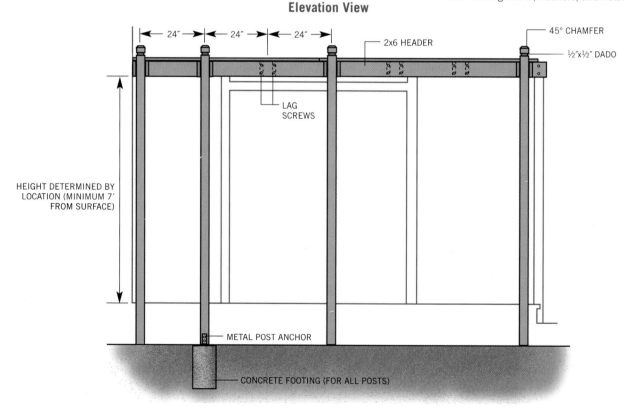

24″   24″   24″   2x6 HEADER   45° CHAMFER   ½″x½″ DADO

LAG SCREWS

HEIGHT DETERMINED BY LOCATION (MINIMUM 7′ FROM SURFACE)

METAL POST ANCHOR

CONCRETE FOOTING (FOR ALL POSTS)

Plan View

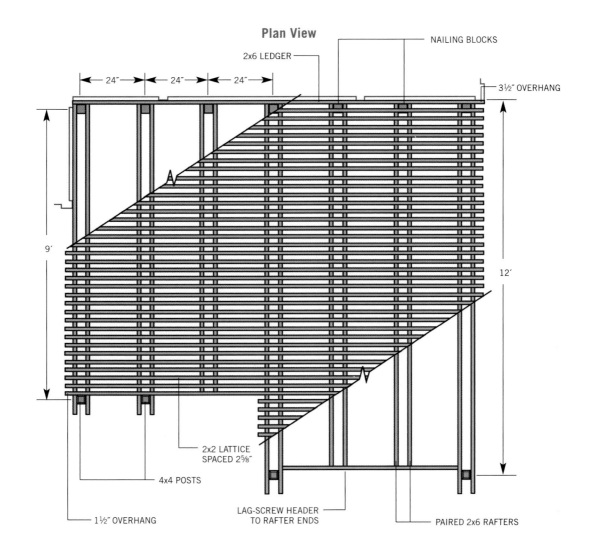

2x6 LEDGER

NAILING BLOCKS

24" 24" 24"

3½" OVERHANG

9'

12'

2x2 LATTICE
SPACED 2⅝"

4x4 POSTS

1½" OVERHANG

LAG-SCREW HEADER
TO RAFTER ENDS

PAIRED 2x6 RAFTERS

6 Cut the header between the installed rafters to length. Predrill clearance holes through the joists. Clamp or otherwise support the header while you drill pilot holes for two ⁵⁄₁₆-by-3-inch lag screws; then install the header with lag screws and washers.

7 Measure and cut all the rafters that fit between the ledger and header, and saturate the end grain with wood preservative. When completely dry, attach them to the nailing blocks at the ledger and the header with lag screws according to the directions above.

8 Using a table saw, rip enough 2-by-4 stock for all the 1½-by-1½-inch trellis cross members (or use stock 2 by 2) and cut them to length. Remove the saw marks with a jointer or surface planer, if available; otherwise, install the cross members cut side up.

9 Sand the trellis cross members, then saturate the exposed end grain at the tops of the posts and the ends of the rafters with wood preservative, apply an oil-based primer, then finish with a 100 percent acrylic-latex exterior paint.

10 Nail a temporary brace across the tops of the two outer rafters to hold them parallel. Install the 2 by 2s with 3½-inch deck screws, using wood blocks to set both the overhang and the space in between the members.

ENTRY SHADE-MAKER

This cooling colonnade runs the length of the house to form a shaded gallery along a brick-lined entryway. The lattice-paneled roof casts shadows across the walkway and helps shelter the house from solar heat gain.
Landscape architect: The Peridian Group.

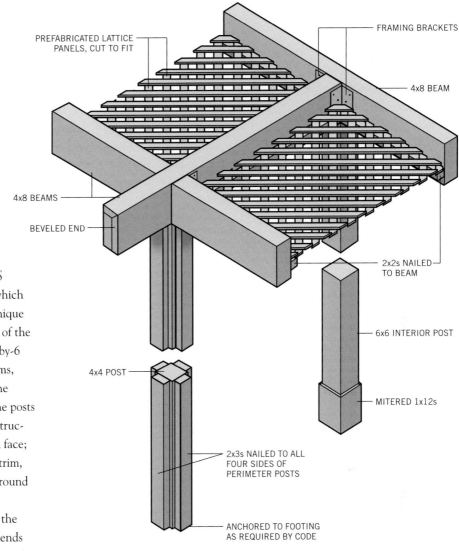

PREFABRICATED LATTICE
PANELS, CUT TO FIT

FRAMING BRACKETS

4x8 BEAM

4x8 BEAMS

BEVELED END

2x2s NAILED
TO BEAM

6x6 INTERIOR POST

MITERED 1x12s

4x4 POST

2x3s NAILED TO ALL
FOUR SIDES OF
PERIMETER POSTS

ANCHORED TO FOOTING
AS REQUIRED BY CODE

DESIGN DETAILS

Unlike most shade structures, which
tend to be free-standing, this unique
patio roof is designed to be part of the
home. A series of 4-by-4 and 6-by-6
posts support the overhead beams,
which in turn are attached to the
house for structural stability. The posts
that form the perimeter of the structure have 2 by 3s nailed to each face;
the interior posts have 1-by-12 trim,
mitered at the corners, nailed around
their bases.

The 4-by-8 beams that form the
ceiling grid are bevel cut at the ends
(you can use a portable circular saw,
but a sliding compound miter saw is
better) and joined together with heavy-
duty metal corner brackets.

Prefabricated lattice panels are set
on 2 by 2s nailed along the beams.

Note from the illustration on this
page that the beam ends extend past
the perimeter posts by 15 inches. The
only exception is at the two outer corners, where diagonal beams extend 24
inches beyond the corner posts.

BUILDING NOTES

Before ordering the lumber, mark the
positions of all the posts. Space the
perimeter posts 4 feet on center and
the interior posts 12 feet on center.
This arrangement yields maximum support without obstructing the flow of
traffic to the front door. If you're building the structure over grass, dig and
pour concrete footings for the posts as
discussed on pages 120–121.

1 First mark the positions of all the posts. Fasten post anchors to the brick (or any other masonry surface) with galvanized screws and lead expansion anchors. Stretch a taut string across the length of the entryway to ensure that the post anchors are perfectly aligned.

2 Cut each post at least 10 inches shorter than the distance from the patio to the underside of the soffit on the house. Attach the 2-by-3 trim to the perimeter posts with galvanized 10d finishing nails. Stand the posts in the post anchors, bracing them plumb with 1 by 4s, and then secure them with galvanized screws.

3 Install the two long 4-by-8 beams that run parallel to the house. Chances are you'll have to use two or three pieces to span the length of the entryway; just make sure that the joint between two beams falls at the center of a post.

4 Next, cut and install the two diagonal beams at each corner so they extend 24 inches beyond the corner posts.

5 Attach a 2-by-8 ledger board to the house so that the bottom edge is level with the top of the posts closest to the house. Securely fasten the ledger with 3-inch decking screws driven through the siding and into the wall studs.

6 Measure and cut 4-by-8 crossbeams to run from the ledger board to the long beam running parallel to the house. Join the beams with metal corner brackets. Fasten the other end of the crossbeams to the ledger with 3-inch decking screws driven in at an angle. Cut and install the second row of crossbeams that fit between the two long beams.

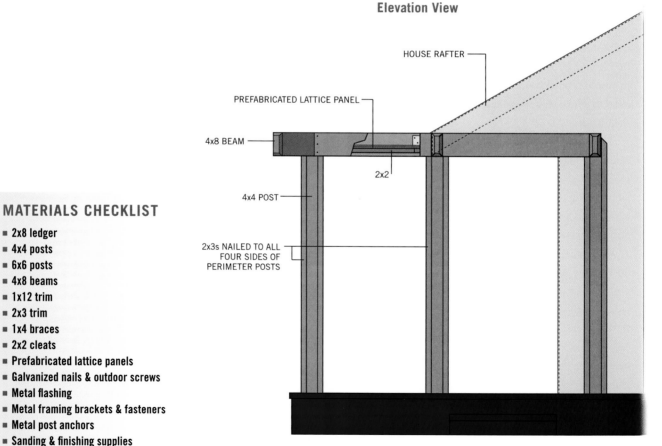

Elevation View

HOUSE RAFTER

PREFABRICATED LATTICE PANEL

4x8 BEAM

2x2

4x4 POST

2x3s NAILED TO ALL FOUR SIDES OF PERIMETER POSTS

MATERIALS CHECKLIST

- 2x8 ledger
- 4x4 posts
- 6x6 posts
- 4x8 beams
- 1x12 trim
- 2x3 trim
- 1x4 braces
- 2x2 cleats
- Prefabricated lattice panels
- Galvanized nails & outdoor screws
- Metal flashing
- Metal framing brackets & fasteners
- Metal post anchors
- Sanding & finishing supplies
- Paint, stain, or wood preservative

Plan View

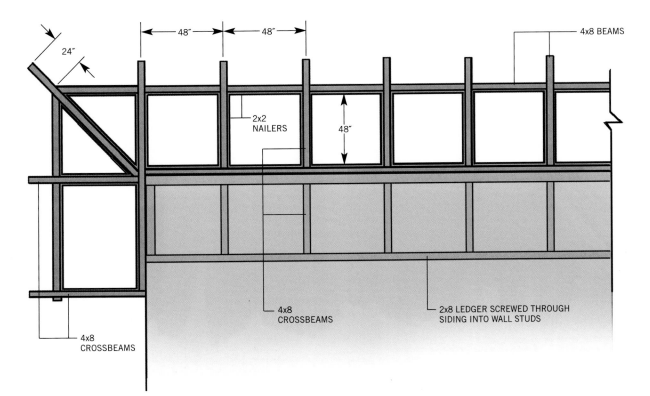

- 24"
- 48"
- 48"
- 4x8 BEAMS
- 2x2 NAILERS
- 48"
- 4x8 CROSSBEAMS
- 2x8 LEDGER SCREWED THROUGH SIDING INTO WALL STUDS
- 4x8 CROSSBEAMS

7 At the ends of the roof, cut 4-by-8 crossbeams to extend at least 4 feet past the corner of the house. Attach the beams to the house with ⅜-inch-diameter-by-6-inch-long galvanized lag screws. Drill a 1-inch-diameter-by-1-inch-deep counter-bore and ⅜-inch-diameter clearance hole through the beams at each wall stud. Use a ratchet wrench to drive the lags into the studs. Tuck metal flashing up under the siding course directly above the beam. Bend it so that it covers the top of the beam and hangs down an inch or so over the front surface. The flashing will prevent water from seeping behind the beam and into the house wall.

8 Cut 2-by-2 nailers to fit around the inside of each square formed by the ceiling grid. Position the bottom edge of the nailers 1½ inches up from the bottom edge of the beams. Attach them with 3-inch decking screws.

9 Using a portable circular saw, cut pre-fabricated lattice panels to fit into the squares in the ceiling grid. Drop them down onto the nailers from above and secure them with 4d galvanized finishing nails. If the lattice splits when you nail it, bore pilot holes first with a ⅛-inch-diameter drill bit.

10 Finally, cut the 1-by-12 base trim for the bottom of the interior posts. Miter the pieces and attach them with 6d galvanized finishing nails.

STYLISH SPACE FRAME

Attached to the house at only one corner, this handsome patio roof is a fitting extension of the home's contemporary-style architecture. The white-painted structure covers nearly 300 square feet of concrete patio and features built-up trim that creates interesting shadow lines along the posts and beams. Landscape architect: Forsum/Summers & Partners.

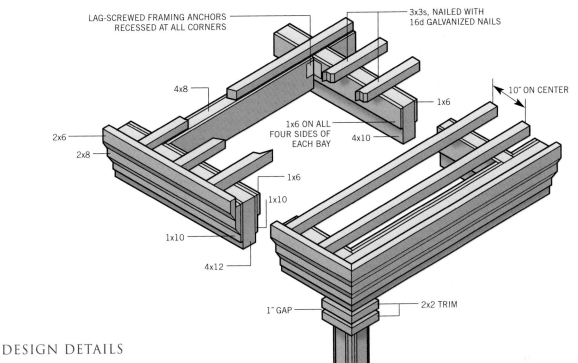

LAG-SCREWED FRAMING ANCHORS
RECESSED AT ALL CORNERS

3x3s, NAILED WITH
16d GALVANIZED NAILS

4x8

2x6

2x8

1x6 ON ALL
FOUR SIDES OF
EACH BAY

1x6

4x10

10" ON CENTER

1x6

1x10

1x10

4x12

1" GAP

2x2 TRIM

6x6 POST

1x4s NAILED TO ALL
FOUR SIDES OF POST

ANCHORED TO FOOTING
AS REQUIRED BY CODE

DESIGN DETAILS

The structure's intricate yet easy-to-build design uses many different sizes of lumber, ranging from delicate 2-by-2 trim to massive 4-by-12 beams. Five 6-by-6 posts support the huge roof beams and the 3-by-3 lattice members that sit on top. Note from the illustration at right that the 3 by 3s are spaced 10 inches on center to permit more sunlight than shade. For a cooler, shadier patio, simply lay out the lattice on 6-inch centers, keeping in mind the additional lumber required.

Three sizes of beams are employed in the roof: 4 by 12s make up the perimeter, which rests on top of the posts. The long main beams, which run parallel to the house, are cut from 4 by 10s. Finally, 4-by-8 crossbeams are set between the main beams, spaced 4 feet on center.

To visually connect the patio roof to the home, partial posts are attached to the corner of the house. The two "half" posts help support the beams where the roof joins the house.

MATERIALS CHECKLIST

- 6x6 posts
- 4x8 beams
- 4x10 beams
- 4x12 beams
- 3x3 trellis stock
- 2x6 fascia
- 2x8 sub-fascia
- 1x4 trim
- 1x6 trim
- 1x10 trim
- 2x2 trim
- Caulking compound, paintable
- Galvanized nails
- Metal post anchors or rebar pins
- Metal framing brackets & fasteners
- Sanding & finishing supplies
- Paint, stain, or wood preservative

Elevation Section View

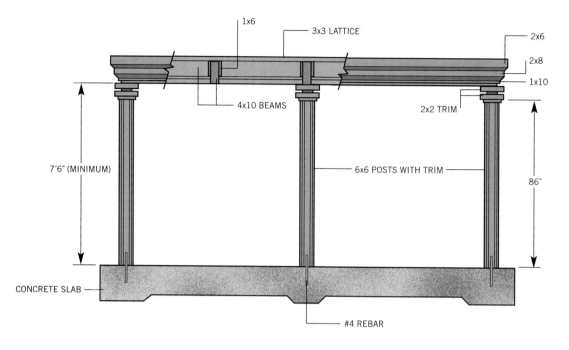

1x6

3x3 LATTICE

2x6

2x8

1x10

4x10 BEAMS

2x2 TRIM

7'6" (MINIMUM)

6x6 POSTS WITH TRIM

86"

CONCRETE SLAB

#4 REBAR

BUILDING NOTES

If building this structure over an existing patio, attach the posts with metal post anchors. Bolt the anchors to the concrete slab with lead anchors and lag screws. Or, if casting a new concrete slab, "pin" the posts to the slab with an 18-inch length of No. 4 (½-inch-diameter) reinforcing bar. Set the bars 12 inches down into the slab and drill 6 inches up into the post bottom, then connect the two with the rebar pin.

Set all the posts and beams first, then begin installing all of the built-up trim pieces. That construction sequence will ensure tight joints and reduce the risk of errors. Apply a coat of paint before assembling the pieces.

1 Cut the 6-by-6 posts to 7 feet, 6 inches long. Attach them to the patio with metal post anchors or rebar pins. If using pins, slip a 5½-inch square of asphalt shingle under each post to prevent them from wicking up moisture. If setting the posts in lawn, dig 18-inch-diameter holes, then follow the instructions on pages 120–121 for casting concrete piers.

2 Cut the 4-by-12 perimeter beams to span across the post tops. Use the longest beams available, but if you must join two timbers to complete a span, be sure the splice falls at the center of a post. Use metal tie-down straps to attach the beams to the posts. Screw right-angle framing brackets to the beams at each of the corners.

3 Next, install the 4-by-10 main beams that run parallel to the house, spacing them 4 feet on center and attaching them to the 4-by-12 perimeter beams with heavy-duty framing brackets. Before screwing the brackets in place, however, mortise out the beams with a hammer and chisel so that the brackets sit flush with the beams. This step is necessary so the brackets won't inhibit the installation of the 1-by trim pieces.

4 Cut the 4-by-8 crossbeams to fit in between the main beams, spacing them 5 feet on center and fastening them in place with heavy-duty framing brackets. Again, recess the brackets so they are flush with the beams.

5 Add the decorative trim to the 6-by-6 posts, starting with the vertical 1 by 4s. Cut the boards to 85½ inches long and nail one to each of the four sides of every post raised ½ inch off the slab. Next, cut the 2-by-2 pieces of cap trim that run around each post, just above the 1-by-4 trim. Miter-cut each piece and nail it to the posts with galvanized finishing nails. Nail up the lower tier of 2-by-2 trim, then the upper tier, leaving a 1-inch space in between the two tiers.

6 Trim out the outside surface of the 4-by-12 perimeter beams, starting with a 1 by 10. Hold the board even with the top of the beam and nail it in place with 6d galvanized finishing nails. Cut to length the 2-by-8 sub-fascia that goes on top of the 1 by 10. Rip a 45-degree angle bevel along the bottom edge of the sub-fascia and fasten the fascia to the 1 by 10 with 12d galvanized finishing nails.

7 Trim out the inside surface of the perimeter beams with 1 by 10s. Then nail 1-by-6 trim boards around the inside of all the squares in the grid formed by the intersecting roof beams. Again, keep all the 1-by trim pieces flush with the top edges of the beams.

8 Next, cut and install the 3-by-3 lattice members. Lay them on top of and per-pendicular to the 4-by-10 main beams, spacing them on 10-inch centers. Fasten them to the beams with 16d galvanized common nails.

9 Conceal the ends of the 3 by 3s with a 2-by-6 fascia. Rip the bottom edge of the fascia at a 45-degree angle bevel and fasten it to the sub-fascia with 12d galva-nized finishing nails. Make sure that the top edge of the fascia is flush with the top of the 3-by-3 lattice members.

10 Fill all the miter joints and seams with a paintable caulk. Allow the caulk to cure, then touch up, as neces-sary, with paint.

Plan View

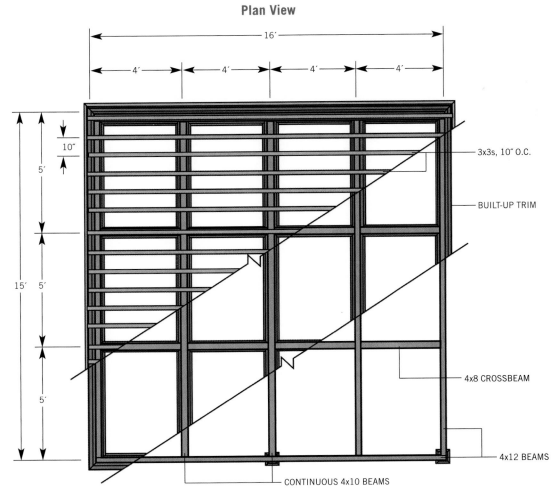

16′

4′   4′   4′   4′

10″

5′

15′   5′

5′

3x3s, 10″ O.C.

BUILT-UP TRIM

4x8 CROSSBEAM

4x12 BEAMS

CONTINUOUS 4x10 BEAMS

POOL-DECK PERGOLA

The main function of this cleverly designed swimming-pool arbor is to provide
shade to the perimeter lounge deck while allowing swimmers to enjoy full sunshine
and a view of the sky. The unique shade structure also creates a crowning touch
to the pressure-treated wood deck that surrounds the 14-foot-diameter aboveground pool. Architect: Jean-Claude Hurni.

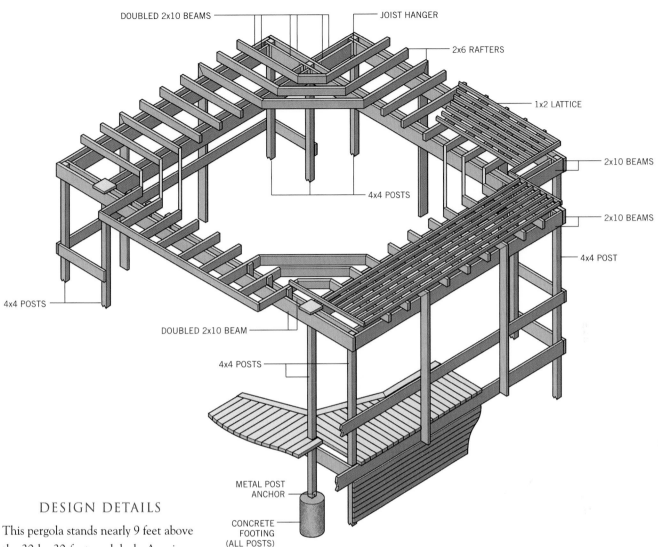

DOUBLED 2x10 BEAMS

JOIST HANGER

2x6 RAFTERS

1x2 LATTICE

2x10 BEAMS

2x10 BEAMS

4x4 POSTS

4x4 POST

4x4 POSTS

DOUBLED 2x10 BEAM

4x4 POSTS

METAL POST
ANCHOR

CONCRETE
FOOTING
(ALL POSTS)

DESIGN DETAILS

This pergola stands nearly 9 feet above the 20-by-20-foot pool deck. A series of 4-by-4 posts supports an overhead framework made up of 2-by-10 beams, 2-by-6 rafters, and 1-by-2 lattice strips. However, the entire center of the pergola is wide open. This design detail—perimeter arbor with open center—lends an intimate, enclosed feeling to the backyard deck.

To create more shade for the lounging area around the pool, space the 1-by-2 lattice strips closer together or replace them with wider 1 by 3s or 1 by 4s. For full shade, lay sunscreen fabric over the top of the lattice. Consider finishing the wood (Step 10) first, then touching up after construction.

BUILDING NOTES

The pergola's ten 4-by-4 posts were installed while the deck was being framed and before the 2-by-4 deck boards were nailed down. Each post sits on top of a concrete footing that extends down to the frost line. The 4 by 4s are attached to the footings with post anchors that were set into place while the concrete was still wet.

If you're adding the pergola to an existing deck, check with your local building inspector. You might be allowed to bolt the posts to the deck's perimeter rim joist or use metal post

anchors to attach the posts directly to the decking.

The tops of the posts are connected by long 2-by-10 beams. Note that in four places the beams are doubled up—placed on either side of the posts. The beams are secured to the post tops with galvanized carriage bolts. Where one double beam meets another at a right angle, joist hangers are used to form a strong, lasting joint.

See Tools and Techniques, beginning on page 102, for complete information on tools and building procedures.

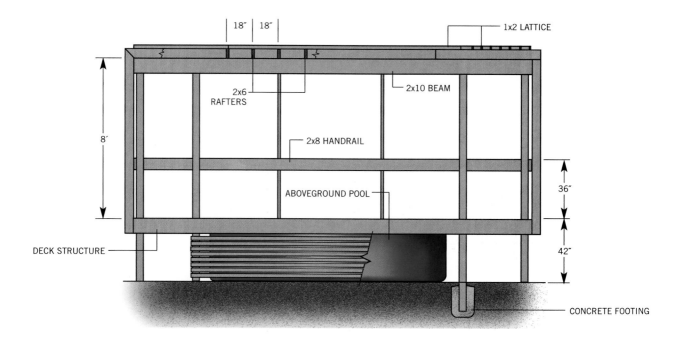

1x2 LATTICE

18″ 18″

2x6
RAFTERS

2x10 BEAM

2x8 HANDRAIL

ABOVEGROUND POOL

8′

36″

42″

DECK STRUCTURE

CONCRETE FOOTING

1 Attach the bottom ends of the 4-by-4 posts to the anchors set in the concrete piers. Use a 4-foot level to check that each post is perfectly plumb, then secure each post by screwing it to one of the deck's 2-by-10 floor joists. If necessary to achieve plumb, slip thin wood shims between each post and joist.

2 Cut the beams to length from 16-foot-long 2 by 10s. If you can't get 2 by 10s long enough to span the length of the pergola, use shorter ones, just make sure that any butt joint falls on the center of a post. Attach the beams to the tops of the posts, starting with the ones that go around the outside perimeter of the pergola. Then install the double beams using carriage bolts and joist hangers as required.

3 After installing the beams, cut the 2-by-6 rafters to length. Note that on the sides and rear of the pergola, the rafters extend 5½ inches past the beams (the width of one 2 by 6) and that on the front of the pergola—the side closest to the house—the rafters are cantilevered 24 inches. Also note that you must trim one end of six rafters on each side to 22½ degrees so you can later install angled rafters that slant at 45 degrees.

4 Position the first rafter 24 inches from the outside beam and space the remaining rafters 18 inches on center. Stand the rafter on edge and secure it to the beams with 2½-inch-long decking screws driven at a sharp angle. If the rafters split when you drive in the screws, bore ³⁄₁₆-inch-diameter pilot holes first.

5 Screw a 2-by-6 fascia across the ends of the rafters that cantilever out from the front of the pergola to stabilize the rafter tails and lend a clean, finished look to the structure. Next, cut the rafter connectors to length and miter-cut both ends of each board to 22½ degrees. Screw these to the rafters you had earlier trimmed to 22½ degrees.

6 Six vertical 2 by 6s extend from the rafters down to the deck's rim joist, two on each side of the pergola and two at the rear. Position each board three rafters in from the corners and screw them in place. These 2 by 6s help bolster the overhead framework and provide solid support for attaching the 2-by-8 handrail.

7 Cut to length the 1-by-2 lattice strips that run across the tops of the rafters on the sides and the back of the pergola. Space the strips 6 inches on center and fasten them to the rafters with 6d galvanized finishing nails.

8 Next, install the 2-by-8 handrail. Measure 36 inches up from the deck boards and snap a level chalk line on the inside surface of each 4-by-4 post and vertical 2 by 6. Align the top of the 2 by 8 with the chalk line and fasten it with 3-inch decking screws. For safety reasons—and perhaps to be in accordance with local building codes—enclose the area below the handrail with 2-by-2 balusters or prefabricated lattice panels.

9 Using a palm-grip orbital sander fitted with 100-grit abrasive paper, smooth over all the exposed corners and edges on the posts and handrail. Also sand smooth any rough spots you find on the deck boards, especially the areas immediately around the nail or screw heads.

10 Apply a clear wood preservative to all wood surfaces, taking care to not drip any into the pool. The preservative will protect the wood not just from the harmful effects of sun and rain but also from the chlorine in the pool water. If you decide to color the pergola, use a semi-transparent stain, but be aware that any pool water splashed onto it will bleach out some of the color.

MATERIALS CHECKLIST

- 4x4 posts
- 2x10 beams
- 2x6 rafters & vertical supports
- 1x2 lattice stock
- 2x8 handrail
- Galvanized nails & outdoor screws
- Metal post anchors
- Metal framing brackets & fasteners
- Galvanized carriage bolts, washers & nuts
- Sanding & finishing supplies
- Paint, stain, or wood preservative

Plan View

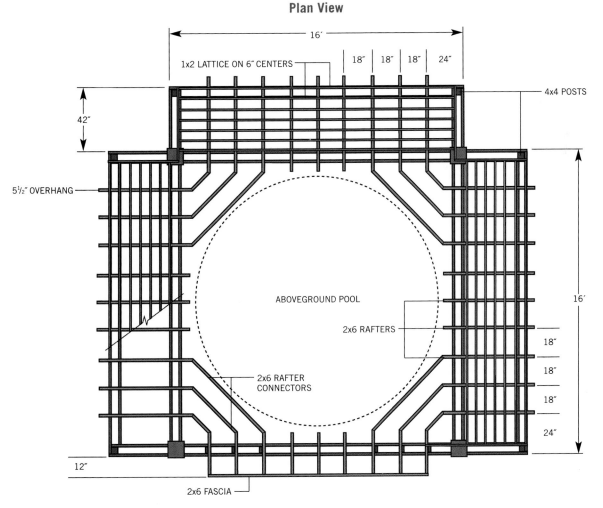

TRADITIONAL TRELLIS

Spanning 47 feet across the patio, this trellis does triple duty—shading a huge patio directly accessible from the dining room (center area), living room, and kitchen. The substantial trellis was carefully designed to be in scale with the architectural details of the house. Architect: Jared Polsky & Associates.

Symmetry and classic lines tie this massive trellis to the home's traditional architecture.

DESIGN DETAILS

Though massive, the dimensions of this trellis—15-inch-diameter columns, 8-by-10 beams, 4-by-7 purlins, and 3-by-3 topmost cross members—can easily be scaled down to suit the size and trim details of a smaller home.

Vines planted in beds at the base of the two double columns reach out across the top of the trellis and up a second-floor balcony railing. They provide dense shade in summer, but when their foliage drops in winter, they allow warming sunlight to pass into the house. The columns stand on a bluestone-capped patio.

Though these homeowners chose a painted finish, if you intend to grow vines on your trellis, a stained finish may be more practical.

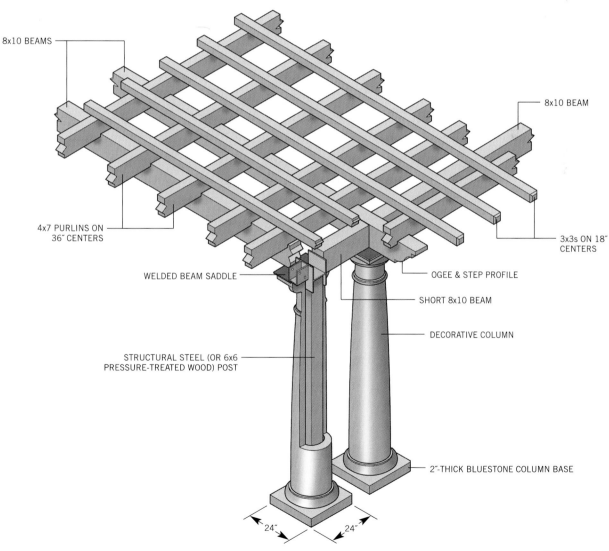

8x10 BEAMS

8x10 BEAM

4x7 PURLINS ON 36" CENTERS

3x3s ON 18" CENTERS

WELDED BEAM SADDLE

OGEE & STEP PROFILE

SHORT 8x10 BEAM

DECORATIVE COLUMN

STRUCTURAL STEEL (OR 6x6 PRESSURE-TREATED WOOD) POST

2"-THICK BLUESTONE COLUMN BASE

24"   24"

BUILDING NOTES

Decorative columns are available as whole columns that fit over structural posts; or they can be split at the mill or on site to wrap around structural posts. A significant advantage of split columns is the relative ease of installation. Steel posts were used for this trellis, but the design could be modified to employ more conventional 6-by-6 pressure-treated wood posts.

The beams are secured to metal anchors mounted with bolts through flashed ledger blocks into the house's framing. To create a perfectly waterproof connection, a nailable waterproof membrane was used to extend copper flashing on all sides.

The short, nonstructural beams extending from the house at the ends were simply scribed and cut to fit into the roof fascia. If your beams similarly need to be scribed, make a plywood template and verify a good joint before tracing the shape onto, and cutting, the beams. Be sure to prime all wood before it is installed.

1 Form the column footings up to grade level and embed the custom-welded post bases in the concrete so their tops are 1¾ inches above the ground. When the concrete is cured, position and plumb each post before welding it to its base.

2 Spread mortar at the base of each post, lay in 2-inch-square bluestone rods, and fill in the area with concrete. Lay a mortar setting bed, then lower the 2-inch-thick, 2-foot-square beveled bluestone column bases down over the posts.

3 Weld the saddles on the tops of the posts. Temporarily position 2 by 4s in the saddles and against the house to ensure that the saddles are perpendicular to the house wall. If whole columns are used, the bases, columns, and caps must be placed over the posts before the welding. Install blocking between the column interior and the posts according to the manufacturer's instructions.

4 Screw the ledger blocks onto the sheathing wall and cover the sheathing with a bituminous membrane. Install copper flashing up the wall and over the top of the ledger, then lap building paper over the flashing. Bolt steel anchors through the blocks into the framing.

5 Cut and sand all the lumber, then brush on or soak in wood preservative and apply primer. As construction progresses, carefully plug or fill all fastener holes. When construction is complete, apply "lifetime" 100 percent exterior acrylic-latex paint.

Elevation View

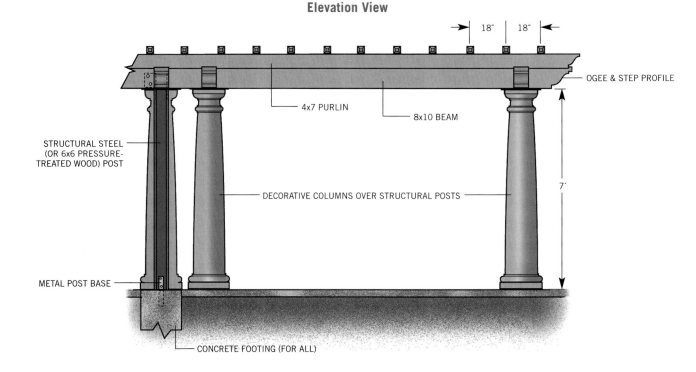

18″ | 18″

OGEE & STEP PROFILE

4x7 PURLIN

8x10 BEAM

STRUCTURAL STEEL (OR 6x6 PRESSURE-TREATED WOOD) POST

DECORATIVE COLUMNS OVER STRUCTURAL POSTS

7′

METAL POST BASE

CONCRETE FOOTING (FOR ALL)

Plan View

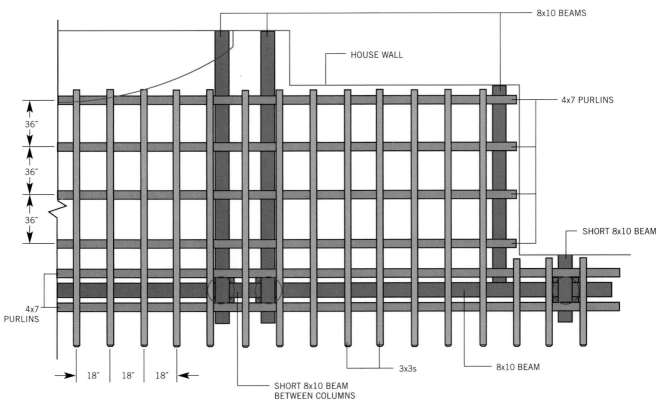

8x10 BEAMS

HOUSE WALL

4x7 PURLINS

36″

36″

36″

SHORT 8x10 BEAM

4x7 PURLINS

18″ 18″ 18″

3x3s

8x10 BEAM

SHORT 8x10 BEAM BETWEEN COLUMNS

6 Using a plywood template, cut and mill the ogee-and-step profile on the outer ends of the beams that extend from the house. Mortise channels in the underside of the beams at the column end and at the house end to accept the steel anchors. Position the beams and locate the clearance holes for the bolts. Counterbore and bore the holes, then install the bolts, nuts, and washers.

7 Attach the short beams between the paired columns to the carrying beams with screws installed diagonally into bored and countersunk holes. Mortise channels in the underside of the remaining beams at both ends to fit over the steel anchors and bolts as before.

8 Lay purlins 36 inches on center across the beams so end joints are centered over a beam. Mark the underside of the purlins where they intersect the beams and cut 1-inch-deep notches in the purlins to fit over the beams. Bore and countersink for screws angled through the purlins into the tops of the beams.

9 Mill the 3-by-3 topmost cross members and chamfer their ends as shown in the illustration on page 95. Install them across the purlins on 18-inch centers with outdoor screws.

10 If split columns, bases, and caps are planned, install them around the posts according to the manufacturer's instructions with waterproof glue and stainless-steel fasteners, making sure there is no direct contact between non-pressure-treated wood and concrete or stone. Flash the tops of the wood caps, leaving the center open for ventilation.

MATERIALS CHECKLIST

- Concrete, #4 rebar & form lumber
- Columns, bases & caps
- 2-inch-by-2-foot-square beveled bluestone column bases
- 2x10 ledger blocks
- Steel posts or 6x6 pressure-treated posts
- 8x10 beams
- 4x7 purlins
- 3x3 trellis stock
- Bituminous membrane
- Metal flashing: copper
- Caulking compound
- Galvanized nails & outdoor screws
- Galvanized lag screws & washers
- Galvanized machine bolts, washers & nuts
- Custom steel post anchors & beam saddles
- Sanding & finishing supplies
- Wood preservative
- Exterior primer
- Acrylic-latex exterior paint

Traditional Trellis **97**

SHADE ARCADE

Here's a fine example of how a patio roof can become an integral part of a home's backyard landscape. This attractive, white-painted shade arbor was custom-designed to complement and enhance an existing brick walkway and patio. It stands close to the house so that all three elements—arbor, patio, and home—work as an integrated design. Landscape architect: Rogers Gardens.

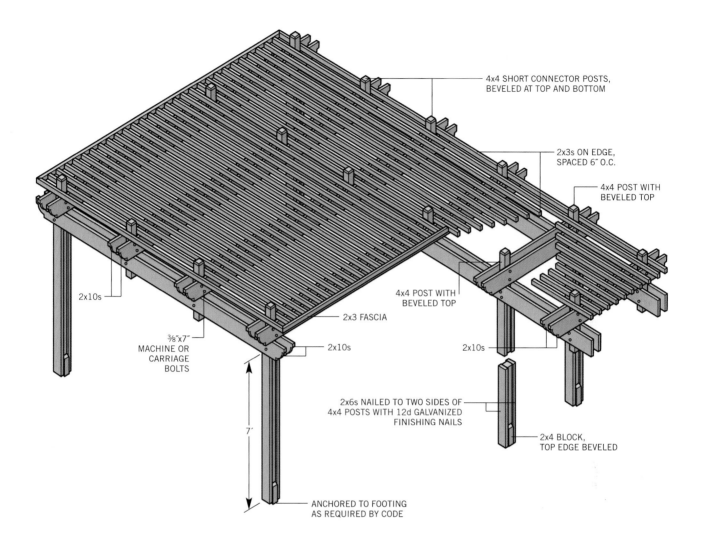

4x4 SHORT CONNECTOR POSTS, BEVELED AT TOP AND BOTTOM

2x3s ON EDGE, SPACED 6" O.C.

4x4 POST WITH BEVELED TOP

4x4 POST WITH BEVELED TOP

2x3 FASCIA

2x10s

2x10s

2x10s

⅜"x7" MACHINE OR CARRIAGE BOLTS

2x6s NAILED TO TWO SIDES OF 4x4 POSTS WITH 12d GALVANIZED FINISHING NAILS

2x4 BLOCK, TOP EDGE BEVELED

7'

ANCHORED TO FOOTING AS REQUIRED BY CODE

DESIGN DETAILS

This free-standing patio roof is anchored by a series of 4-by-4 posts that support an overhead arbor made up of crisscrossing 2-by-10 beams and 2-by-3 lattice boards. Note from the illustration above that two sides of each 4-by-4 post are trimmed with 2 by 6s. This treatment adds dimension to the posts, while creating a strong shoulder upon which the beams can rest.

Short connector posts are inserted between the beams along the spans between the main posts. These 29-inch-long posts strengthen the arbor without compromising its free-flowing, open design. All of the beam-to-post connections are secured with 7-inch-long galvanized machine or carriage bolts.

BUILDING NOTES

Start by determining where to set the posts. You can attach them directly to the patio with metal anchors or set them in concrete footings alongside the patio. If you decide to pour concrete footings, dig the holes at least 12 inches in diameter and follow the instructions on pages 120–121. Each 4-by-4 post must be 9 feet, 1 inch tall, measured from level ground or patio surface to the post top. Before setting the main posts, chamfer their top ends using a power miter saw or radial-arm saw. Chamfer both ends of each of the connector posts.

For the beams, select straight, kiln-dried lumber in the longest lengths available. If you can't span a distance with a single board, join two boards together at the center of a post.

See Tools and Techniques, beginning on page 102, for complete information on tools and building procedures.

1 Paint (or stain) all of the lumber before cutting, then coat the ends after. If you decide not to paint or stain, apply a clear wood preservative to all surfaces.

2 Set the 4-by-4 posts in place and brace them plumb. Cut two 2-by-6 trim boards to 7 feet long for each post. Attach two of the boards to opposite sides of each post, flush with the patio, using 12d galvanized finishing nails or 3-inch decking screws.

3 Cut a 2 by 4 to 8 inches long. Bevel its top end to 45 degrees, using a power miter saw or radial-arm saw. Then, nail the block between the 2-by-6 trim boards at the base of a post. Cut and install more blocks to each side of every post.

4 Next, cut the 2-by-10 beams that run parallel to the house. Again, if necessary, be sure that all splice joints fall at the center of a post. Before installing the beams, use a saber saw to cut a decorative ogee profile in their ends. Lightly hand-sand the beam ends smooth with a piece of 80-grit abrasive paper.

5 Set the beams on top of the 2-by-6 trim boards fastened to the posts. Clamp or tack-nail the beams to the posts, check for level, then use a ⅜-inch-diameter spade bit with an extension to bore clean through the two beams and post. Tap a ⅜-inch-diameter-by-7-inch-long galvanized machine bolt with washer or carriage bolt through each hole. Slide a washer onto the bolt end, then thread on a hex nut. Tighten the nut with a socket wrench. Repeat with all beams that run the same direction.

Elevation View

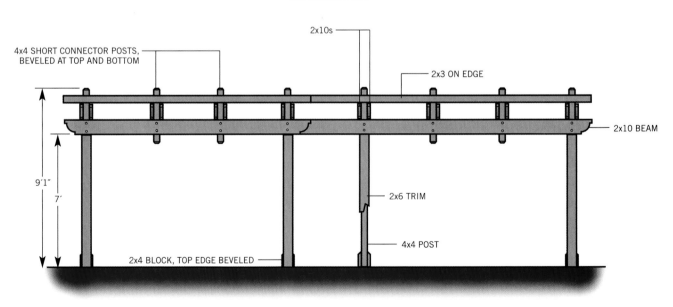

4x4 SHORT CONNECTOR POSTS, BEVELED AT TOP AND BOTTOM

2x10s

2x3 ON EDGE

2x10 BEAM

9'1"

7'

2x6 TRIM

4x4 POST

2x4 BLOCK, TOP EDGE BEVELED

6 Cut to length all of the connector posts. Chamfer both ends of each post, using a power miter saw or radial-arm saw. Slip the 4-by-4 connectors between the 2-by-10 beams at 4-foot intervals so that 4 inches of post protrudes below the beams. Bore clearance holes and secure the connectors with 7-inch-long machine or carriage bolts.

7 Install the second tier of 2-by-10 beams on top of the first beams but perpendicular to the house. Attach them to the main posts and connector posts with 7-inch-long machine or carriage bolts.

8 Cut to length the 2-by-3 lattice boards that run across the second tier of beams. If necessary, make sure all splice joints fall at the center of a supporting beam. Space the boards 6 inches on center and set them on edge. Fasten them to the beams with 8d finishing nails—one nail into each beam—driven in at an angle (toenailed). If the 2 by 3s split as you drive in the nails, bore $\frac{3}{32}$-inch-diameter pilot holes first. Use 3-inch decking screws to attach the lattice boards that abut a post. Note: If the ends of the 2 by 3s are irregularly aligned, snap a chalk line across the ends and trim them straight.

9 Measure and cut 2-by-3 fascia boards to cap the ends of the lattice. Nail the fascia to the ends of the lattice boards using 12d galvanized finishing nails. Drive the nails below the surface with a nailset.

10 Go back with a paintbrush and touch up any spots of bare wood with fresh paint, stain, or wood preservative. Apply a coat of finish to all fasteners.

Plan View

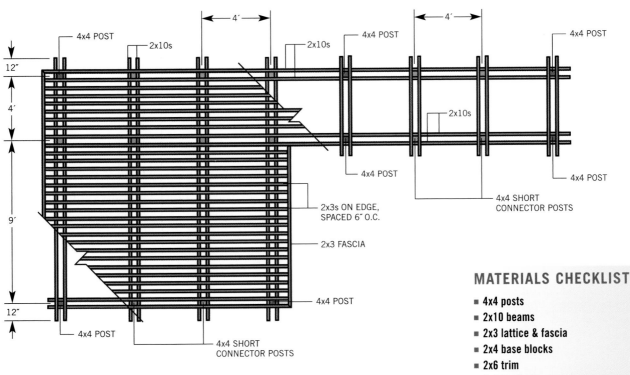

MATERIALS CHECKLIST

- **4x4 posts**
- **2x10 beams**
- **2x3 lattice & fascia**
- **2x4 base blocks**
- **2x6 trim**
- **2x8 handrail**
- **Galvanized nails & outdoor screws**
- **Metal post anchors**
- **⅜-x7-inch galvanized machine bolts, washers & nuts**
- **Sanding & finishing supplies**
- **Paint, stain, or wood preservative**

for do-it-yourselfers, the aroma of fresh sawdust is just one of the rewards of launching into a new building project. But beyond this simple pleasure, converting a stack of lumber into a handsome garden structure offers a sense of real accomplishment and a terrific addition to your yard.

If building an outdoor structure sounds a bit intimidating, you'll be happy to know that many designs are relatively simple, requiring skills and tools that fall within the repertoire of most handy homeowners. These designs often employ a systems approach, with components that you build repeatedly to complete the structure.

Whether you intend to build a structure yourself or you just want to develop a workable design, this chapter can be your guide. Explore the entire chapter before finalizing your design or starting to build. You'll need a clear understanding of specifications in order to determine beam sizes, post spacing, and other important structural details (for more about planning, see the chapter beginning on page 4).

Although these pages will guide you through the building process from the ground up, designing an overhead structure often takes place in the reverse order. A particular type of roofing material will demand a method of support by rafters, which, in turn, will dictate certain sizes and spacing of beams, posts, and other structural components.

tools and

techniques

MATERIALS

Shopping for lumber, fasteners, and other materials can be daunting. If the choices don't overwhelm you, some of the prices probably will. The best way to get through the lumberyard or home-improvement center with a minimum of confusion and expense is to go prepared. Know what to look for—types, sizes, and grades—and how materials are sold. The following material-buying primer can help you accomplish this.

When choosing materials, become familiar with the information beginning on page 12 regarding lumber and other materials.

LUMBER

Regardless of the material you choose for the roof surface of your outdoor structure, its framework will likely be constructed from wood. Following are some lumber-buying basics.

SPECIES Woods from different species of trees have varying properties. Redwood, cedar, and cypress heartwoods (the darker part of the wood, cut from the tree's core) have a natural resistance to decay. This characteristic, combined with their natural beauty, makes these woods a favorite for decking, natural-finish lath-type roofing, and similar applications. But these woods are usually more expensive than ordinary structural woods such as Douglas fir, yellow southern pine, and western larch. So landscape professionals often specify these woods—or treated woods—for the structural parts of an overhead and save premium woods for where beauty is important.

Lumber is divided into softwoods and hardwoods, terms that refer to the origin of the wood, not its hardness (though most hardwoods tend to be harder than softwoods). Softwoods come from conifers, hardwoods from deciduous trees.

As a rule, softwoods are much less expensive, easier to tool, and more readily available than hardwoods, so softwoods are chosen for nearly all wood construction outdoors.

LUMBER GRADES At the mill, lumber is sorted and identified by name, and, in many cases, the species and the grading agency.

Generally, lumber grades are determined by a number of factors: natural growth characteristics or blemishes such as knots; defects caused by milling errors; and techniques used for drying and preserving wood that affect strength, durability, or appearance.

When it comes to lumber grades, you get what you pay for. In most cases, higher grades cost far more than lower grades. The fewer the knots and other defects, the pricier a board. To save money on a project, pinpoint the lowest grade suitable for each component.

Structural lumber and timbers are

Grades of redwood range from rough and knotty (LEFT) to clear (FAR RIGHT). Higher grades are more attractive and, because they contain higher percentages of heartwood, are more decay resistant.

LINEAR VS. BOARD FEET

Lumber is sold either by the linear or board foot. The linear foot, commonly used for small orders, considers only the length of a piece. For example, 20 2 by 4s, 8 feet long, would be the same as 160 linear feet of 2 by 4.

The board foot is a common unit of measure for volume orders, and lumberyards often quote prices per 1,000 board feet. A piece of wood 1 inch thick, 12 inches wide, and 12 inches long equals 1 board foot. To compute board feet, multiply the thickness in inches by the width in feet by the length in feet. For example, a 1-by-6 board 10 feet long would be computed: 1 inch x ½ foot (6 inches) x 10 feet = 5 board feet.

When ordering lumber, however, you still must list the exact dimensions you need so your order can be filled correctly.

Pressure-treated lumber is grade-stamped according to its appropriate uses; look for the American Wood Preserver's Bureau (AWPB) mark.

rated for strength. The most common grading system includes the grades Select Structural, No. 1, No. 2, and No. 3. For premium strength, choose Select Structural. Many lumberyards sell a mix of grades called No. 2-and-Better. Other grading systems used for some lumber classify wood according to the grades Construction, Standard, and Utility, or as a mixture of grades called Standard-or-Better.

Redwood is usually graded according to appearance and percentage of heartwood. Clear All heart is the best and the most expensive. B heart, Construction heart, and Merchantable heart are, in descending order of quality, typical grades of pure heartwood.

Cedar grades, starting with the highest quality, are Architect Clear, Custom Clear, Architect Knotty, and Custom Knotty, but don't indicate whether or not the wood is heartwood.

PRESSURE-TREATED LUMBER

Though redwood and cedar heartwoods are naturally resistant to decay and termites, most other woods soon rot and weaken when in prolonged contact with soil or water. Common lumber such as southern pine and western hem-fir can be factory-treated with chemical preservatives that guard against rot, insects, and other sources of decay. Termed "pressure-treated," this lumber is less expensive than redwood or cedar, and in some regions, more readily available. It can be used for structural members such as posts, beams, and rafters.

Pressure-treated wood is available in two "exposures." For lumber that will be close to or touching the ground, the Ground Contact type is required. Use the Above Ground type for other applications. The American Wood Preserver's Bureau, which governs the treatment industry, grade-stamps preservative-treated lumber according to its appropriate uses.

Treated lumber does have drawbacks. Unlike redwood and cedar, which are soft and therefore easy to cut and drive fasteners into, treated wood can be hard, brittle, and prone to warp and twist. Moreover, some people object to the greenish color (though applying paint or a semi-transparent stain can mask this) and the staplelike incisions that usually cover the surface (some newer types come without marks).

The primary preservative used for pressure-treated lumber contains chromium, a toxic metal. Wear safety glasses and a dust mask when cutting this type of lumber and wear gloves when handling it for prolonged periods. Never burn scraps of treated lumber.

STANDARD LUMBER SIZES Lumber is normally stocked in lengths from 6 to 20 feet and in a broad range of widths and thicknesses. Various size categories are given different names—boards, dimension lumber, lath, and so forth. For more about some of these, see pages 12–13. Note that the actual sizes of surfaced boards and dimension lumber are less than those suggested by their names, as shown in the chart below. The difference is the amount reduced by shrinkage during drying and removed by planing.

To figure the minimum sizes for supporting loads, consult the chart on page 13. Keep in mind that these are minimums—you can select larger sizes for appearance or to handle excessive loads. Of course beefier sizes also increase your lumber bill.

STANDARD DIMENSIONS OF SOFTWOODS

Nominal (surfaced)	Actual
1x2	¾″ x 1½″
1x3	¾″ x 2½″
1x4	¾″ x 3½″
1x6	¾″ x 5½″
1x8	¾″ x 7¼″
1x10	¾″ x 9¼″
1x12	¾″ x 11¼″
2x2	1½″ x 1½″
2x3	1½″ x 2½″
2x4	1½″ x 3½″
2x6	1½″ x 5½″
2x8	1½″ x 7¼″
2x10	1½″ x 9¼″
2x12	1½″ x 11¼″
4x4	3½″ x 3½″
4x6	3½″ x 5½″
4x8	3½″ x 7¼″
4x10	3½″ x 9¼″
6x8	5½″ x 7¼″

FASTENERS

Nails, bolts, screws, and metal connectors are used to join materials and strengthen the joints of patio roofs and gazebos. The following will guide you in choosing appropriate fasteners.

NAILS Nails are sold in 1-, 5-, and 50-pound boxes, or loose in bins.

Use hot-dipped galvanized, aluminum, or stainless-steel nails outdoors; other types will rust. In fact, even the best hot-dipped galvanized nail will rust over time, particularly at the exposed nail head, where the coating is battered by your hammer. Stainless-steel or aluminum nails won't rust, but they are far more expensive than galvanized nails, and aluminum nails bend easily.

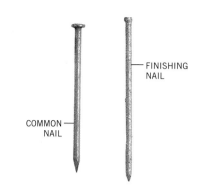

You can choose between common and finishing nails. The common nail, favored for construction, has an extra-thick shank, a broad head—and holds the best. Where you don't want a nail's head to show, choose a finishing nail (after you drive it nearly flush, sink the slightly rounded head with a nailset).

SCREWS Though they're more expensive than nails, coated or galvanized screws offer several advantages. They don't pop out as readily as nails, and their coating is less likely to be damaged during installation. With screws, you don't have to worry about hammer dents. Screws also are easier to remove than nails when repairs are required.

Galvanized deck screws are surprisingly easy to drive into softwoods such as redwood or cedar if you use an electric drill or screw gun with an adjustable clutch and a Phillips screwdriver tip. Drywall screws (so-called multipurpose screws), usually black in color, come in smaller sizes than deck

screws but are not very resistant to the elements. These two types of screws are not rated for shear (or hanging) strength, so opt for nails, lag screws, or bolts to fasten rafters to beams or ledgers and to join posts to beams.

The lag screw (also called a lag bolt) is a heavy-duty fastener with a square or hexagonal head; it is driven with a wrench or a ratchet and socket. Before driving a lag screw, predrill a lead hole about two-thirds the length of the lag screw, using a drill bit that's 1/8 inch smaller than the lag screw's shank. Slide a washer onto each lag screw before driving it.

Choose screws that are long enough to penetrate about twice a top member's thickness (for example, use 2½-inch screws to join two 2 by 4s or 2 by 6s). Screws are sold loose, by the pound, or in up to 25-pound boxes; the bigger the box the more substantial your savings will be.

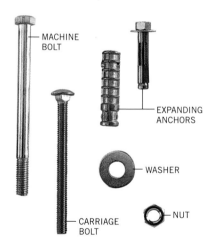

BOLTS For heavy-duty fastening, choose bolts. Most are zinc-plated steel, but aluminum and brass ones are also available. Bolts go into predrilled holes and are secured by nuts. The machine bolt has a square or hexagonal

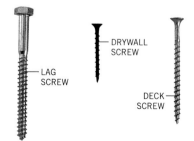

HOW LONG IS A 16-PENNY NAIL?

Though a box of nails may indicate nail size in inches, "penny" (abbreviated "d") is the unit of measure classically applied to a nail. As you can see by this table, the higher the penny, the longer the nail.

NAIL	LENGTH
4d	1½″
5d	1¾″
6d	2″
7d	2¼″
8d	2½″
10d	3″
12d	3¼″
16d	3½″
20d	4″

Why the term "penny," and why is it abbreviated "d"? When this term was first applied, it indicated the cost of 100 hand-forged nails; for example, 100 large nails cost 16 cents. The abbreviation "d" comes from the Latin denarius, a type of Roman coin (a silver denarius was about a soldier's pay for one day).

head, a nut, and two washers; it must be tightened with a wrench at each end. The carriage bolt has a self-anchoring head that digs into the wood as the nut is tightened.

Expanding anchors allow you to secure wooden members to a masonry wall or slab floor. They feature expanding sleeves that grip the hole firmly when the bolt is driven home.

Bolts are classified by diameter (⅛ to 1 inch) and length (⅜ inch and up). To give the nut a firm bite, select a bolt ½ to 1 inch longer than the combined thickness of the pieces to be joined.

It's better to make a connection with several small-diameter bolts or lag screws rather than with fewer large-diameter bolts. The number and size will depend on the width of the lumber being joined.

FRAMING CONNECTORS Metal framing connectors are often used in construction to make joining materials easier and to strengthen joints. They are used throughout almost all of this book's projects, but are often hidden from view by wood components.

You'll find many types of framing connectors in sizes designed to fit most standard-dimension rough and surfaced lumber. A welder or metal shop can fabricate odd sizes or decorative specialty supports.

When using framing connectors, be sure to use the size and type of nails specified by the manufacturer—they are generally shorter and fatter than standard nails.

Joist (and rafter) hangers, probably the most familiar metal connectors, are used to secure the butt joints between ceiling joists or rafters and the load-bearing beam, joist header, or ledger.

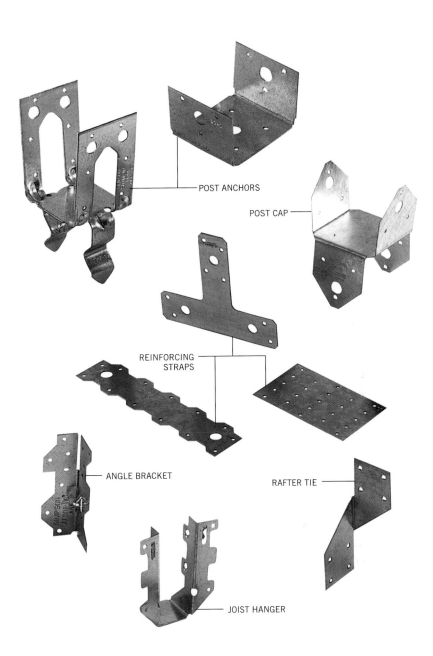

POST ANCHORS

POST CAP

REINFORCING STRAPS

ANGLE BRACKET

RAFTER TIE

JOIST HANGER

Some joist hangers have metal prongs that can be hammered into the side of the joist (the connection to a beam must be made with nails).

Post anchors secure the base of a load-bearing post to a concrete foundation, slab, or deck. In regions where there's likely to be standing water caused by heavy rains, builders typically choose an elevated post base that raises the post 1 to 3 inches above the base.

Post caps top a post to join the post to a beam. They also can strengthen a splice connection between two beams.

"Framing anchors" is a catch-all term for a variety of connectors. Hurricane or seismic anchors or rafter ties eliminate the need for toenailing (joining two members together by nailing at an angle) between rafters and a wall's top plate; reinforcing angle brackets create solid joints between any two members that cross; and reinforcing straps strengthen post-to-beam joints.

TOOLKIT

For building patio roofs and gazebos, you'll need an assortment of basic carpentry tools. You won't necessarily need all of the tools discussed here, but these will handle the major tasks of most projects. Though you can get by with hand tools for most jobs, power tools will let you do the job more quickly, easily, and accurately, especially if the structure is large.

HAND TOOLS

A collection of basic tools is outlined below. You may already have most or even all of these, but if you're shopping, this information can point you in the right direction.

STEEL MEASURING TAPE A simple 6-foot tape may be all you need for a small structure, but for larger jobs, consider a ¾- or 1-inch-wide tape that's 16 or 25 feet long. Wider tapes won't twist and buckle, so the longer the distance you need to measure, the wider the tape you should consider.

SQUARE A square helps you draw straight lines across lumber to be cut; it also helps you check angles on assembled pieces of a structure. A basic, fixed try square will do, but an adjustable combination square is more useful. A sliding T-bevel helps you lay out angles.

HAMMER Choose a 12-to-16-ounce curved-claw hammer for general work and a 20-ounce straight-claw model for framing (it packs a bigger wallop for longer nails). The face should be smooth, not serrated, to minimize any dings you might make in the wood.

PLUMB BOB & MASON'S LINE Most overheads require a reference point when you're lining up posts or transferring layout lines from the ground to overhead beams. To accomplish this work, you'll want to employ a plumb bob and mason's line.

LEVEL A carpenter's level, typically 2 feet long, helps check a structure for both level and plumb; a 4-foot mason's level is even handier—and more accurate. To check level across a very long distance, consider using a line level or water level (essentially a water-filled tube); new electronic versions emit a beep when the levels at both ends align.

CHISEL & BLOCK PLANE Though not really essential, these basic carpentry tools can be handy for cleaning up saw cuts and joints. A plastic-handled, metal-capped butt chisel can be driven by a hammer.

CROSSCUT SAW Unlike the specialized rip saw (used for "ripping" wood in line with the grain), a crosscut saw is designed to cut boards across their widths; it's also handy for cutting plywood. A good choice is a 26-inch blade with 8 points per inch. For finer work, you might want a backsaw, which is stiffer than a crosscut saw and has finer teeth (it's usually used with a miter box; see below).

COPING SAW Cutting curves is the coping saw's business. The wider the saw's throat, the farther in from a board's edge you can cut. An inexpensive saber saw, also known as a jigsaw (see page 110), does the same type of cutting but is easier to use and much more versatile.

MITER BOX Made from wood, metal, or plastic, this troughlike frame has various standard angles cut in its sides to guide the saw blade. You can use a backsaw, standard crosscut saw, or hacksaw with most versions.

WRENCH An adjustable wrench is good for many bolt and nut sizes, but is not

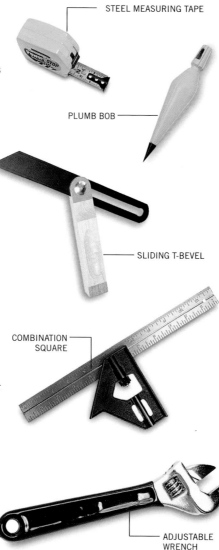

STEEL MEASURING TAPE

PLUMB BOB

SLIDING T-BEVEL

COMBINATION SQUARE

ADJUSTABLE WRENCH

as precise or easy to handle as a box or open-end wrench. A ratchet-and-socket set is even easier to use and may be required to reach into a counter-sunk bolt hole while tightening.

CLAMPS When you feel you need an extra pair of hands, often what you really need is a clamp. Clamps hold things stationary where you want them, and they're also essential for holding certain parts together while glue dries. C-clamps are the old standby; bar clamps have a longer reach. The spring clamp, which looks like an oversized clothespin, is inexpensive and great for small jobs.

POWER TOOLS

The following portable power tools make large projects go a lot faster and easier; in the hands of the average do-it-yourselfer they also produce better results than hand tools. There are big, expensive stationary power tools to be had—and if you have access to a table saw, radial-arm saw, or band saw, you'll find they're great for some stages of building an overhead or gazebo.

ELECTRIC DRILL & BITS This power tool has all but replaced hand drills and screwdrivers (at least when more than a couple of screws are involved). Look for a ⅜-inch reversible drill; cordless models are very handy, particularly when working a distance from electrical receptacles. To bore holes up to ½ inch in diameter, use standard twist bits; for larger holes, use spade bits. A carbide-tipped masonry bit can tackle stucco siding with no problem. When fitted with a Phillips-head tip, the drill is equally handy as a power screwdriver, but you'll need a variable-speed model

GOGGLES

SAFETY GLASSES

DUST MASK

LEATHER-REINFORCED COTTON WORK GLOVES

RUBBER GLOVES

WORKING SAFELY

Before you begin work, make sure you have the necessary safety equipment on hand. Wear goggles, safety glasses, or a face mask when operating power tools or using any striking tool. Wear a respirator to prevent breathing harmful vapors (such as those from oil-based finishes). A disposable painter's dust mask can protect you from breathing heavy sawdust; it's essential when cutting pressure-treated lumber. Also wear earmuff hearing protectors or earplugs when operating power tools for any length of time. A hard hat offers protection when you're working beneath an overhead or working with others in close quarters.

Wear all-leather or leather-reinforced cotton work gloves to handle wood; wear rubber gloves when applying finishes or other caustic products. Sturdy work boots, especially the steel-toed sort, will protect your feet from dropped tools or lumber.

When using a new tool, always read the owner's manual carefully and follow all safety directions. To guard against shock, power tools must be either double-insulated or grounded. Double-insulated tools, which contain a built-in second barrier of protective insulation, offer the best protection; they are clearly marked and should not be grounded (they have two-pronged plugs only).

Since most of your work will probably transpire outdoors, take special precautions against shock. A ground-fault circuit interrupter (GFCI), either portable or built into the outlet, is essential; it will cut the power with lightning speed if there's a leak in current.

COMPOUND
MITER SAW

or the screws will strip. Models with an adjustable clutch prevent screws from being driven too deep.

PORTABLE CIRCULAR SAW This does the same job as a handsaw but much more quickly. Equipped with a combination blade, it can handle crosscuts and rip cuts (cutting in line with the grain). The 7¼-inch size is standard.

MITER SAW Also called a chop saw, the miter saw is the power version of the good old backsaw and miter box. It excels at making clean, accurate angle cuts; if your project entails a lot of angles or requires a lot of detail work, consider renting one. A 10-inch miter saw is standard. So-called compound miter saws cut angles in two directions at once, a feature that's sometimes handy for rafters or fancy trim. Sliding miter saws can cut stock up to about a foot wide.

ROUTER The electric router makes short work of grooves, rabbets (grooves along an edge), and the decorative edge treatments that can spice up a basic project—chamfers (bevels) and roundovers (rounded edges), for example. Look for a router rated at least 1 horsepower.

SABER SAW ("JIGSAW") This is the electric version of the coping saw; it can be used for both straight and delicately curved cuts. Unlike a coping saw, the saber saw can make cuts well away from an edge, and it even makes interior "pocket" cuts if you drill an access hole first. Choose the right blade for the job: thin, fine-tooth blades for tight curves, beefier ones for rougher, straighter cuts.

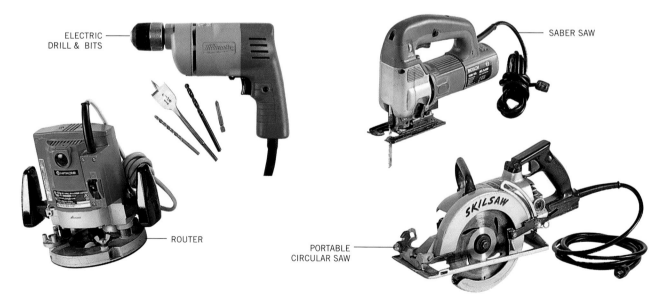

ELECTRIC
DRILL & BITS

SABER SAW

ROUTER

PORTABLE
CIRCULAR SAW

BUILDING TIPS

A typical overhead or gazebo requires a number of basic carpentry skills. Here you'll find a few special techniques that can make the going easier. If you're completely unfamiliar with tasks such as measuring and cutting lumber and hammering nails, check out Sunset's *Basic Carpentry* book.

CUTTING WITH SAWS

Every project in this book involves cutting wood. Here are a few helpful tips for the types of cutting involved in building outdoor structures.

CUTTING STRAIGHT Regardless of whether you're using hand tools or portable power ones, sometimes it's hard to get a really straight cut. One solution is to clamp on a guide; any straight board or plywood piece will do.

Use a straightedge to guide your handsaw or portable circular saw. If you're using a power saw, first figure the distance from the edge of the saw's baseplate to its blade, then space the straightedge this distance from the line you are cutting.

DEEP CUTS Cutting all the way through a 4-by-4 post can be awkward. If you're using a handsaw, first mark the cutting line across the board, then,

guiding the pencil with your square, extend it down both sides. Use the side lines to keep your saw on track. With a circular saw, you can only cut about half the depth of the board at once. Finish the cut with a handsaw (using the existing cut as a guide) or flip the 4 by 4 over and make another cut from the bottom, carefully matching saw kerfs (cuts).

CUTTING ANGLES To cut angles, first mark the line using a combination square (45-degree angles only) or a sliding T-bevel. If it's a standard angle, such as a 30 degree or 45 degree, you can cut it using a miter box and handsaw; otherwise, you'll need to cut freehand. With a circular saw, either cut freehand (which can be tricky) or clamp on a guide, remembering to allow for the distance from baseplate to blade. Odd angles are a piece of cake for the power miter saw.

A miter box makes 45-degree and 90-degree cuts across small stock an easy job.

CUTTING CURVES Cut curves freehand with either a coping saw or a power saber saw. If the curve is uniform, lay it out using a compass or a French curve, or by plotting it on paper, then cutting it out to make a template. If you are making more than one matching piece—say, decorative rafter tails or knee braces—cut the first one to your satisfaction, then use it to lay out the rest. Some saber saws include circle-cutting guides—the saw tracks around a central point. When cutting concentric circles (like a doughnut shape), make the inside cut first so you'll have plenty of stock left to support the saw during the outside cut.

DECORATIVE CUTTING The decorative details in some of this book's projects are best done with an electric router. Most edge details—such as chamfers, rabbets, and roundovers—are fashioned

A straightedge helps guide a circular saw.

A saber saw cuts accurate curves with speed.

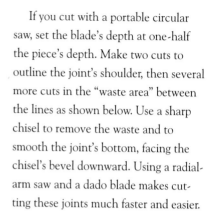

Decorative edge details are the router's specialty. Shown here, from top to bottom, are a chamfer, rabbet, and roundover.

with corresponding bits; these all come with pilot bushings that guide the bit along an edge. Do this sort of detailing before assembling the structure. You can also cut rabbets using a table saw and dado blade.

BASIC JOINERY

Most patio roof and gazebo projects call for simple butt joints; trim pieces are sometimes mitered or lapped. All three joints are shown below right.

BUTT JOINTS Butt joints have standard 90-degree ends. If one piece overlaps the other, driving nails or screws is easy. However, if the pieces join in a T and you can't drive fasteners from behind, they can be awkward to join. Traditional "toenailing" can be exasperating, since the part being secured tends to move off-line as you hammer. Screws are a bit easier to work with, especially if you drill angled pilot holes first. Clamps and blocks can also hold pieces in line. However, framing connectors or L-brackets are easier to use at these junctions, and they also make for a stronger joint; if you don't like the way they look, you can paint them.

MITER JOINTS Miter joints are cut at 45-degree angles. End miters (like those you see at the corners of picture frames) are pretty straightforward. Edge miters are difficult to cut by hand unless the stock is narrow enough to fit upright in a miter box; for these, a sliding or compound miter saw, radial-arm saw, or table saw may be in order. You can also use a circular saw's bevel (side-tilt) adjustment, but cuts made this way are often imprecise.

LAP JOINTS Lap joints call for other techniques. A half-lap has a notch or groove cut in one piece and the other piece sits inside this notch. A full-lap joint, where both pieces are of equal thickness, joins corresponding notches, each one-half the total depth. It's a lot of work to cut these with a handsaw.

If you cut with a portable circular saw, set the blade's depth at one-half the piece's depth. Make two cuts to outline the joint's shoulder, then several more cuts in the "waste area" between the lines as shown below. Use a sharp chisel to remove the waste and to smooth the joint's bottom, facing the chisel's bevel downward. Using a radial-arm saw and a dado blade makes cutting these joints much faster and easier.

DRILLING FOR FASTENERS

Sometimes you really need to drill a clean, straight hole, especially if it will be highly visible. Two problems may crop up: first, the hole may not be exactly perpendicular; and second, the back of the hole (where the drill bit exits the wood) may splinter.

DRILLING STRAIGHT You can usually drill a fairly straight hole simply by eyeballing the drill bit's angle as you go; if

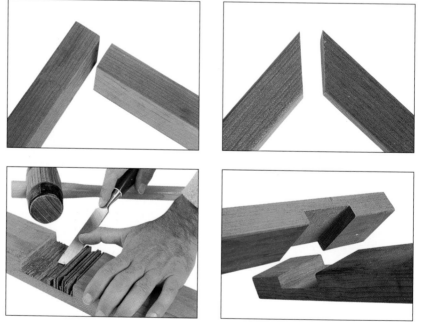

CLOCKWISE FROM TOP LEFT: Butt joint; miter joint; lap joint; to shape a lap joint's notch, make repeated saw cuts, then clean out the "waste" with a sharp chisel.

To countersink a machine bolt, first drill a large, shallow hole for the fastener's head and washer, then drill a smaller shank hole to go clear through the wood.

you like, place a square next to the drill to help you judge. If the hole really needs to be straight and you don't have a drill press, consider using a portable drill guide, which is designed to keep the drill perpendicular.

PREVENTING SPLINTERING You can solve the problem of ragged exit holes two ways. Temporarily attach a wood scrap behind the joint and drill clear into it to prevent splintering; or begin to drill through the piece and stop when the bit's tip starts to protrude, then flip the piece and finish drilling from the back.

DRILLING PILOT HOLES Deck and drywall screws have sharp points and aggressive threads, so you shouldn't need to drill pilot holes to drive them into redwood or other softwoods. But if they aren't cooperating or if you're splitting the wood when fastening near an end, choose a drill bit slightly smaller than the screw and drill a pilot hole about three-quarters the screw's length.

COUNTERSINKING Lag screws and machine bolts often look better if countersunk; that is, their heads are

below the wood's surface. Use a spade bit to bore the countersunk hole for the head first; size it just slightly larger than the fastener's washer and drill just deeper than the length of the fastener's head. Then drill a second, smaller pilot hole for the fastener itself through the center of the countersink hole. For lag screws, make this second pilot hole the same diameter as the smooth shank between the screw threads and head. Drill the hole about two-thirds the length of the screw.

DRIVING LAG SCREWS & BOLTS Start the lag screw with a few hammer blows, then drive it tight with a wrench or ratchet. If it won't go in, make the pilot hole longer. For bolts, drill a hole just slightly larger than the shank (the bolt must slide freely inside it) all the way through the joint.

Use two wrenches to secure a machine bolt: one on the head and another on the nut to keep it from twirling. Carriage bolts require just one wrench, on the nut; the head should stay put.

WORKING WITH CONCRETE

Typically posts for overheads rest on piers embedded in poured concrete footings. Although many people think concrete is just "cement," it is actually a combination of portland cement, sand, aggregate (usually gravel), and water. Bagged dry, ready-mixed concrete is an expensive alternative to buying the ingredients separately but far more convenient for small jobs. The standard 90-pound bag makes $\frac{2}{3}$ cubic foot of concrete, enough to fill one posthole or to fill a 4-inch-deep, 16-inch-square area. If your project is fairly large, order materials in bulk and mix them yourself, either by hand or with a power mixer.

You can dig postholes with a pick and shovel, but using heavier equipment will save time and effort. A posthole (clamshell) digger works well in hard or rocky soil. However, posthole diggers are awkward to use for holes deeper than 3 feet because the hole's sides make it difficult to spread the tool's handles.

Concrete ingredients include sand, gravel, cement, and water.

PARTS & PIECES

Though there are many ways to build a patio roof or gazebo, most utilize the same basic components—a foundation, posts or walls, beams, rafters (or joists), and some type of roofing. The typical components of patio roofs and gazebos are shown here.

Patio roofs and gazebos are typically supported by a foundation, usually a series of footings and piers. The foundation distributes a structure's weight on the ground and anchors the struc-

ture against settling, erosion, and wind lift. The foundation also isolates the posts (or walls) from direct contact with the ground, reducing the chance of decay and insect infestation.

Sometimes a gazebo or overhead can sit directly on a patio slab or deck without an additional foundation; it all depends on the structure's weight and the deck's construction or the slab's thickness (see page 119). Your local codes will be the determining factor.

GAZEBOS

Like a patio roof, a gazebo is typically supported by a foundation, but in this case, the foundation is often a concrete slab or patio.

As a base for the posts and/or walls, a sill of treated 2-by lumber is fastened to the slab with expansion anchors. The posts are fastened to the sill with post anchors. The tops of the posts are secured to the beams by metal hangers or post caps; alternately, you can toe-nail through the beams into the posts. Knee braces ensure a more rigid structure. The rafters radiate outward from a central hub and are joined to the top ends of the posts or the beams. The gazebo may be capped with either solid or open roofing.

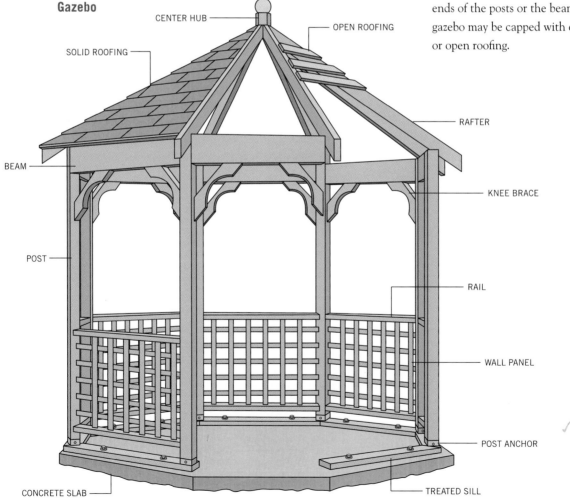

Gazebo

CENTER HUB

OPEN ROOFING

SOLID ROOFING

RAFTER

BEAM

KNEE BRACE

POST

RAIL

WALL PANEL

POST ANCHOR

CONCRETE SLAB

TREATED SILL

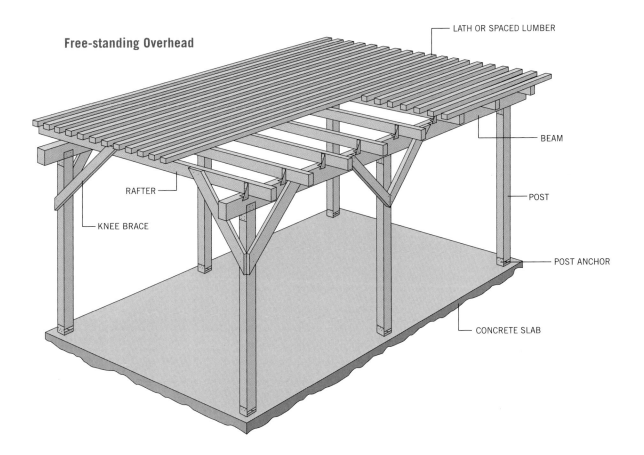

Free-standing Overhead

LATH OR SPACED LUMBER

BEAM

POST

POST ANCHOR

CONCRETE SLAB

RAFTER

KNEE BRACE

PATIO ROOFS

A patio roof or overhead may be free-standing, such as the one shown above, or it can be attached to the house with a ledger, as show at right. In either case, the structure is supported by a series of posts, which can be continuations of deck posts, or they can rest on concrete paving or piers and footings.

If you're adding an overhead to an existing deck, bolt the overhead posts to the deck's substructure, placing them directly above or adjacent to the deck posts. The overhead posts support rafters. If the overhead is attached to the house, the ledger takes the place of a beam, supporting the rafters directly. Overhead rafters can be left open or they can be covered with any one of a number of materials.

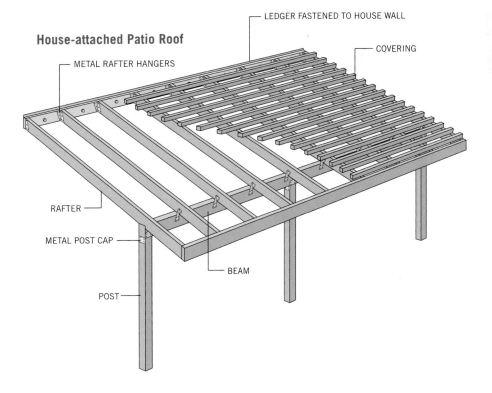

House-attached Patio Roof

LEDGER FASTENED TO HOUSE WALL

COVERING

METAL RAFTER HANGERS

RAFTER

METAL POST CAP

POST

BEAM

STEP-BY-STEP PATIO ROOF

The illustrated steps on this page provide a brief overview of the building sequence for a free-standing overhead. You'll find more detail about working with posts, beams, rafters, and roofing on the following pages.

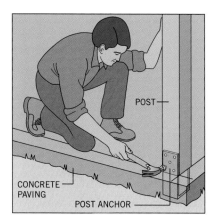

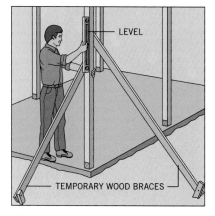

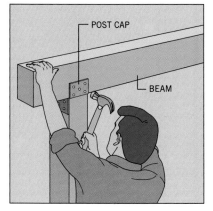

1 Set the posts in anchors embedded in a concrete slab or in concrete footings or concrete piers after cutting the posts to length and nailing post caps on top. Hold the posts vertical and nail anchors to them. For more about posts, see page 124.

2 To plumb the posts, place a level on two adjacent sides of each post. Secure the post position with temporary wood braces nailed to wood stakes driven into the ground.

3 Position a beam on top of the posts that will support it. Check that the post is vertical and that the beam is level, shimming it if necessary. Then nail the post caps to the beam. For more about beams, see page 124.

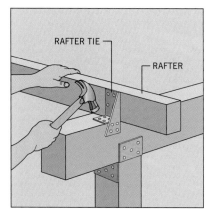

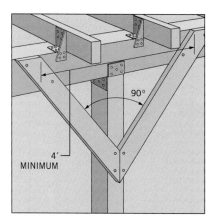

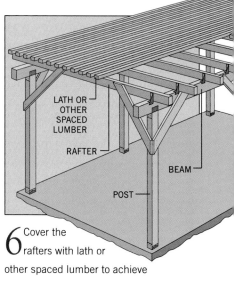

4 Set and space the rafters on the tops of the beams and secure them with rafter ties, as shown, or by toenailing them to the beams. If the span warrants, install bracing. See page 127 for more about installing rafters.

5 Nail or bolt 1-by-4 or 1-by-6 braces, with the ends cut at 45 degrees, between the beams and posts. Cut the braces long enough so that the beam ends are at least 2 feet from the post caps. Be sure the structure you create is sturdy and safe. Bracing is discussed on page 126.

6 Cover the rafters with lath or other spaced lumber to achieve the desired amount of shading. Nail the roofing material to the rafters. For more about roofing, see page 130.

INSTALLING A LEDGER

A house-attached patio roof takes advantage of the house's support by connecting one side onto a ledger mounted horizontally to the house. The ledger, usually a 2 by 6, often supports one end of the patio roof rafters. The ledger should be attached before the foundation is built. Locating and mounting it is normally a fairly easy process.

LOCATING THE LEDGER The best place to mount a ledger is on the wall under the eaves, fastened through the siding to the house framing. Measure carefully to make sure there'll be room for the rafters between the ledger and eaves line.

If the eaves aren't high enough to allow for proper headroom, support the patio roof by mounting it in one of the other ways shown on page 118. Don't fasten it to the eaves or rafter tails or it might exert undue leverage on the house rafters.

FASTENING THE LEDGER To fasten to a wood-frame (including stuccoed) house, lag-screw the ledger to the wall studs on a single-story house and to the upper-floor framing on a two-story house. The lag screws must go through the exterior siding (or roofing) and it is essential they penetrate well into the framing members.

To fasten to wood framing, first level the ledger at the desired height. If your house has wood siding, temporarily nail the ledger in place; otherwise, just brace it securely. Recheck for level and drill lag-screw pilot holes through the ledger and siding into the studs or into the floor framing. Finally, lag-screw the ledger in place with ½-by-5½-inch lag screws, spaced every 16 inches (or as specified by local codes).

To fasten to masonry walls, first mark a level line across the wall for the

Rafter-to-House Connections

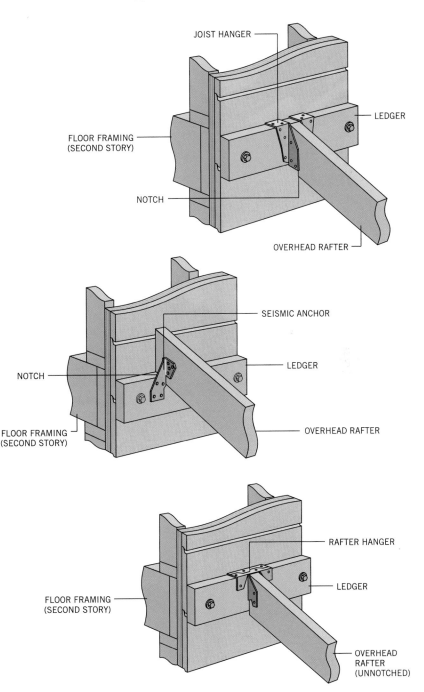

JOIST HANGER

LEDGER

FLOOR FRAMING (SECOND STORY)

NOTCH

OVERHEAD RAFTER

SEISMIC ANCHOR

LEDGER

NOTCH

OVERHEAD RAFTER

FLOOR FRAMING (SECOND STORY)

RAFTER HANGER

LEDGER

FLOOR FRAMING (SECOND STORY)

OVERHEAD RAFTER (UNNOTCHED)

ledger's top edge and drill holes in the wall for expanding anchors. Insert the anchors and, holding the ledger in place, tap with a hammer to mark the anchor locations on the back face of the ledger. Remove the ledger and drill bolt holes in it where the anchors have made dents. Then push or hammer the ledger onto the bolts, recheck level, add washers and nuts, and then tighten.

FLASHING THE LEDGER Unless it's protected from rain by eaves or a solid roof, a ledger fastened directly to a house should be capped with L-shaped galvanized metal flashing and caulked along the top flange to prevent moisture penetration. This must be done before the rafters are placed.

Make a form for bending the sheet-metal flashing by clamping two 2 by 4s together on each side of the metal; then hammer to form the metal. Cap the ledger with the flashing, caulk the top flange to the wall, then nail the flashing to the ledger and house siding with galvanized roofing nails. If the house has shingle or lapped siding (or if you're fastening to the roof), don't caulk the top edge—instead, slip it up under the bottom edge of the shingles or siding. Caulk the nail heads.

Rafter-to-Roof Connections

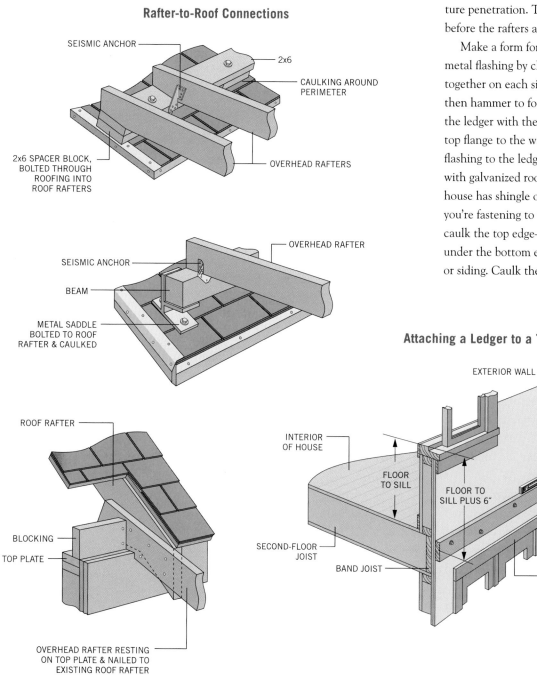

Attaching a Ledger to a Two-story House

THE FOUNDATION

A gazebo or patio roof must stand on a solid foundation such as a concrete slab or a series of concrete footings and piers. Foundation requirements are set by local codes; a steel-reinforced concrete footing that extends 6 inches below the frost line, as shown on page 121, is typical for patio roofs and gazebos with built-up floors. The footing supports a poured-in-place or precast concrete pier, which in turn supports a post. The placement of footings and piers is determined by the post locations, which are determined by the beam and rafter spans. For more about these see page 13.

Some gazebos have concrete-slab floors that, if thick enough, can serve as the structure's foundation. For more about these, see page 120.

Paging through this book's projects, you'll find a variety of ideas for creating solid yet attractive foundations for overheads and gazebos. The best foundations are often those that are also the least noticeable.

Once you've determined the size and layout of your overhead's foundation, transfer the measurements to the ground, deck, or patio with chalk or by driving stakes into the ground.

For precise placement of posts, set up batterboards as shown at right. These will allow you to adjust and maintain taut perimeter lines.

If you're building a patio roof that will be attached to a house wall, hang a plumb bob from the ledger where one corner of the patio roof will meet the wall. Make a mark on the wall about 12 inches off the ground and drive a nail partially into the wall. Repeat this procedure at the other corner where the patio roof will meet the wall.

Set up batterboards about 18 inches beyond where the outside corners of the patio roof will be. Stretch a mason's line or string from the nails in the wall to the batterboards that are parallel to the wall.

To square the corners of your layout, measure 6 feet along the wall from one string toward the other string and make a mark. Measure 8 feet out from the wall and cross the tape measure over the string. Then hook the end of the tape measure onto a nail at the wall where you have made the first mark. Adjust the string until the diagonal is exactly 10 feet. Hammer a nail into the batterboard at that spot and attach the string to it. (The triangulation method of squaring corners works in any multiple of 3-4-5—for example, 6-8-10 or 9-12-15. For maximum accuracy, use the largest ratio possible.)

Repeat this procedure at the other corner where the patio roof will meet the wall. Finally, attach a third string to the batterboards that run perpendicular to the house to form the patio roof's outside edge, equidistant from the wall at both ends.

Remember that these lines indicate the perimeters of the posts and footings, not their centers.

For a free-standing overhead, use the same method, just start from stakes in the ground instead of at the house wall.

BUILDING ON A SLAB OR DECK

Codes may allow setting the overhead directly on an existing slab or deck. If the slab isn't thick enough for the weight of the overhead, you'll have to either pour new footings around the

Setting Up Batterboards

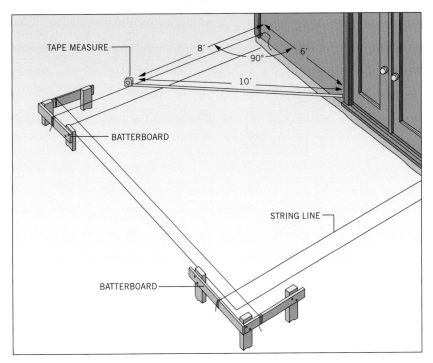

TAPE MEASURE

8'

90°

6'

10'

BATTERBOARD

STRING LINE

BATTERBOARD

Anchoring a Post to a Slab

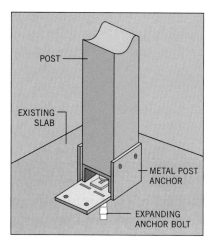

POST

EXISTING
SLAB

METAL POST
ANCHOR

EXPANDING
ANCHOR BOLT

slab's perimeter or break out sections
and pour deeper footings.

BUILDING OVER AN EXISTING SLAB

To fasten an overhead directly to an
existing slab, secure each post in a post
anchor. Standard post anchors are sized
to capture rough and surfaced 4-by-4,
4-by-6, and 6-by-6 posts. (Other sizes
can be specially fabricated.)

Using a masonry bit, drill a hole in

the concrete, centered for each anchor,
to receive a ½-inch expanding anchor
bolt. Insert the anchor bolt, place the
post anchor, add a washer and nut, and
tighten with a wrench. When it's time
to place the post, you just cut the end
square, place it in the post anchor, and
nail the anchor to the post.

BUILDING OVER AN EXISTING DECK

Posts can be bolted or lag-screwed to
the sides of existing deck beams, joists,
or other heavy structural members.
Or, post anchors can be lag-screwed
through decking to a joist or beam.

INSTALLING
FOOTINGS & PIERS

You can pour footings and piers together or place ready-made piers into wet
concrete footings, as shown opposite.

FORMING A CONCRETE FOOTING Dig
a properly sized hole to 6 inches below
the frost line or at least 12 inches deep.
Tamp the bottom of the hole and add

any necessary steel reinforcing bar
(normally required if piers are more
than 1 foot high), then add 6 inches of
gravel. Fill the hole with fresh concrete
to within 3 inches of ground level.

If you're going to pour piers and
footings together, make forms for the
piers from scrap wood. For cylindrical
piers, use specially manufactured fiber
tube forms. These tubes can be sawed
to any length and have a coated inner
surface that makes peeling them off
later an easy job.

MIXING CONCRETE To mix your own
concrete, use 1 part cement, 2 parts
clean river sand, and 3 parts gravel
(maximum 1 inch in diameter and specially washed for concrete mixing).
Add clean water, a little at a time, as
you mix. The concrete should be plastic, not runny.

Use a shovel or hoe to mix the concrete on a wooden platform or in a
wheelbarrow. Spread two shovelsful of
sand and one of cement on the mixing
surface. With a rolling motion, mix
until the color is even. Then add three
shovelsful of gravel and continue mixing until the color is even. Finally,
scoop out a hole in the middle of the
dry ingredients and add three quarts
of water.

Work around the puddle, slowly
rolling the dry ingredients into the
water. Avoid slopping the water out of
the wheelbarrow.

If the batch is too stiff, add water, a
cup at a time, and continue mixing
until it's right. If the mixture is too
soupy, add small amounts of sand and
gravel a little bit at a time (do not add
even the smallest amount of concrete,
which, at this stage of mixing will
change the consistency radically).

Fastening a Post to a Deck's Structure

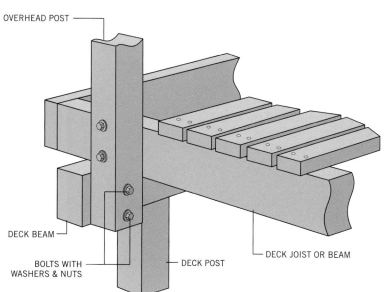

OVERHEAD POST

DECK BEAM

BOLTS WITH
WASHERS & NUTS

DECK POST

DECK JOIST OR BEAM

Cylindrical Fiber Form

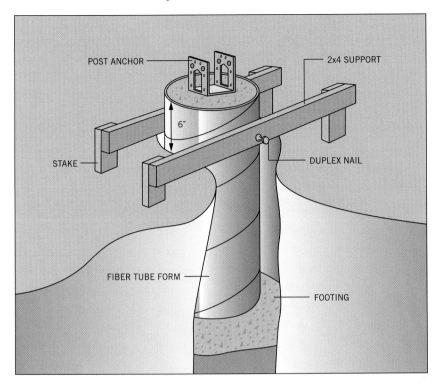

POST ANCHOR

2x4 SUPPORT

6″

STAKE

DUPLEX NAIL

FIBER TUBE FORM

FOOTING

If you're using a machine-powered mixer, estimate the 1:2:3 proportions of cement, sand, and gravel by shovelsful. Add 2½ gallons of water per half-bag of cement. Mix until right, then pour.

POURING FOOTINGS & PIERS Pour the footings first and insert any steel reinforcing required. If you're pouring piers with the footings, fill the forms with concrete, then use a screed or

straight board to level the wet concrete flush with the tops of the forms. Immediately embed metal post anchors, aligning them with your string lines. While the concrete is still plastic, hold a carpenter's level against a short length of post placed in the post anchors and adjust for plumb. Be careful not to move the anchors out of alignment.

If you're using ready-made piers, choose the type with integral metal post anchors. Soak the piers with a hose, then place them on the footings five to ten minutes after the footings have been poured, when the concrete is stiff enough to support them. Then, with the post anchors properly aligned with your string lines, level the piers in both directions.

Allow the concrete to cure for at least a week before removing the forms; cover the poured piers with newspaper and keep them damp during this time. Cover the footings with soil to prevent the concrete from drying too quickly.

Ready-made Pier on a Footing

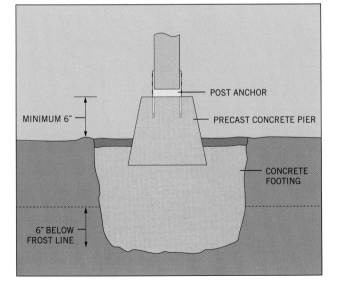

POST ANCHOR

PRECAST CONCRETE PIER

MINIMUM 6″

CONCRETE FOOTING

6″ BELOW FROST LINE

Contiguous Pier

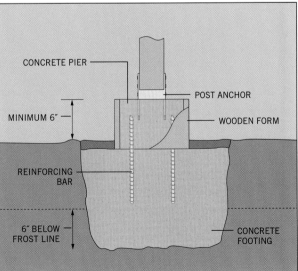

CONCRETE PIER

POST ANCHOR

MINIMUM 6″

WOODEN FORM

REINFORCING BAR

6″ BELOW FROST LINE

CONCRETE FOOTING

CASTING A CONCRETE SLAB

For some gazebos and similar structures, you'll need to form and cast a concrete-slab floor. The steps that follow will guide you through this job. Mix the concrete as discussed on pages 120–121, but in this case make the formula 1 part portland cement, 2½ parts sand, 2½ parts gravel aggregate, and ½ part water.

Excavate the area for a 4-to-6-inch-deep bed of gravel and a 4-inch-thick concrete slab. Place the gravel in the excavated area and rake it until flat and level.

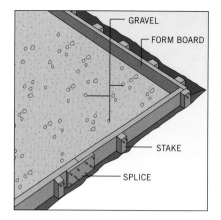

1 Position temporary form boards with their inner faces along the perimeter lines you've laid out for the structure and so that their top edges are level with what will be the top of the slab. Fasten the boards to 1-by-3 or 2-by-2 stakes and to each other at the corners with galvanized screws or box nails.

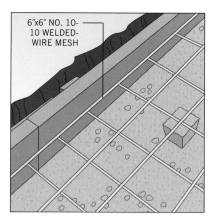

2 To strengthen the slab, lay 6-inch-square No. 10-10 welded-wire mesh or crisscross ½-inch reinforcing bar on 12-inch centers. Support the mesh or reinforcing bar about 2 inches above the base, using small pieces of brick or block.

3 Before placing the concrete, thoroughly dampen the soil or gravel. Beginning at one corner, place and spread the concrete. Work the mix up against the form and compact it into all corners with a shovel or mortar hoe by pushing (not dragging) the concrete. Don't overwork the material—doing so will cause the aggregate to sink to the bottom.

4 Move a straight 2 by 4 across the top of the forms to level the concrete, using a zigzag, sawing motion. Fill any voids with more concrete.

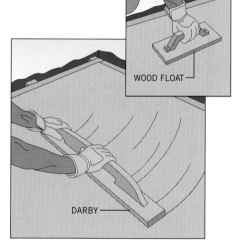

5 Move a darby (which you may want to rent) in overlapping arcs, then repeat with overlapping straight, side-to-side strokes. Keep the tool flat, but don't let it dig in. After the water sheen has disappeared from the concrete but before the surface has become really stiff, smooth it once more with a wood or magnesium hand float.

FINISHING WOOD PARTS

To protect a wooden outdoor structure and preserve its beauty, you'll want to apply a water repellent, a semi-transparent or solid-color stain, or paint. Whatever product you choose, try it on a sample board first. And always read product labels; some products should not be applied over new wood, and others may require a sealer first. With most projects, you will want to finish the wood components before assembling the structure. The most efficient way to do this is before you have cut the parts. After cutting, you finish the ends. Then touch up the structure after it is assembled.

Water repellents (water sealers) help keep wood from warping and cracking. They may be clear or slightly tinted; the clear sorts do not color the wood but let it fade gradually to gray. You can buy either oil- or water-based products, many of which include UV blockers and mildewcides.

Don't use clear-surface finishes such as spar varnish or polyurethane on outdoor lumber. Besides being costly, they wear quickly and are very hard to renew.

Available in both water- and oil-based versions, semi-transparent stains contain enough pigment to tint the wood's surface with just one coat while still letting the natural grain show through. You'll find grays and wood tones as well as products to "revive" an unpainted structure's natural wood color or dress up pressure-treated wood.

To cover a structure in a solid color, you can choose either stain or paint. Stains for siding or decking are essentially thin paints that cover the wood grain completely. For custom tints, you can usually mix any paint color you choose into this base.

Paints cover wood in an opaque coat of muted to vibrant color. Because they hide defects so thoroughly, they let you use lower grades of lumber. Most painters recommend a two-step procedure for outdoor structures: first apply an alkyd- or oil-based prime coat, then follow it with one or two topcoats of water-based (latex) enamel. Ideally, the primer should cover all surfaces of the lumber (including the inner faces of built-up posts, beams, or rafters), so prime before assembly. Apply topcoats after the structure is completed.

Heavy-bodied stains may be either brushed or sprayed on; paint can be applied with a brush, roller, or spray gun. It's easiest to spray complex shapes like lath and lattice.

POWER SPRAYERS

Power sprayers can save you considerable time, and while there is some disagreement among professionals whether sprayed surfaces are as durable as brushed surfaces, most agree that if the sprayer is used properly the finish will last just as long as one created with a brush or roller.

The most common paint sprayers are known as airless sprayers and are made in a variety of sizes. In general, sprayers are particularly useful for painting deeply textured, hard-to-reach, or multipiece surfaces that have many nooks and crannies.

FROM TOP TO BOTTOM: Unfinished redwood; with clear water sealer; tinted oil-based repellent; gray semi-transparent stain; and red solid-color stain.

POSTS & BEAMS

Overheads are most commonly supported by posts or columns, a variety of which are shown below. Large-dimension-lumber beams run from post to post or, in some cases, from post to ledger. The beams support the roof rafters or joists, which in turn hold the roofing material. Minimum sizes of posts and beams are set by engineering requirements and are strictly governed by local building codes (see page 13).

Built-up Beam

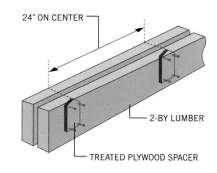

24″ ON CENTER

2-BY LUMBER

TREATED PLYWOOD SPACER

POSTS & COLUMNS

Posts are generally made from solid lumber, built-up lumber, decay-resistant treated poles (available from lumber or landscaping dealers), steel, or a combination of these materials. In some cases, columns take the place of posts.

Wooden posts offer plenty of opportunity for detailing. You can rout them, cut them, build up interesting profiles, or nail on decorative pieces that add visual interest. For ideas, see this book's project section as well as the illustrations below.

Wherever wooden posts or columns will touch the ground, be sure the wood is pressure treated or decay resistant. Metal post anchors that raise posts about an inch off the ground allow for the use of standard lumber, though it's still a good idea to seal the posts' ends with a preservative.

BEAMS

Beams can be solid lumber or built up from lengths of 2-by lumber nailed together with ½-inch pressure-treated plywood spacers in between (this method forms a 3½-inch-thick beam, equal to the width of a 4-by post). A built-up beam is easiest to handle because you can assemble it near its final destination, but making one involves a little more labor. Where highly visible, a single, solid beam generally looks better.

If you must assemble a long, built-up beam from shorter lengths, stagger the joints between successive layers and plan for each of these joints to fall directly over a post. Be sure the crowns of the pieces are aligned on the same side and face upward. (The crown is the "high" side of a curve or warp along the edge of a board.)

Post Possibilities

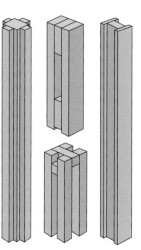

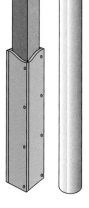

Treated poles are decay resistant. Avoid using recycled telephone poles or others that may have been treated with creosote, a harmful chemical.

Prefabricated columns are generally non-structural, but most are designed to conceal a structural wood or steel post inside.

Built-up lumber can serve as an attractive alternative to solid lumber.

Solid lumber may be surfaced, rough, or re-sawn. Routed grooves, rounded corners, or trim add interest.

Steel posts can be covered with wood; they're generally specified only for extreme loads.

ERECTING POSTS & BEAMS

Accurately measuring post heights is critical when building an overhead: you cannot achieve a stable, properly aligned substructure without precise post measurements. The construction examples discussed here are for attached overheads with beams and rafters; if your design is different, adjust the directions accordingly.

For an attached overhead, measure, cut, and erect the posts farthest from the house first. For a free-standing roof, begin with the corners, then erect the intermediate posts.

Measuring posts for a free-standing roof differs in only one respect from measuring for a house-attached roof. With the attached roof, you've already defined the roof height at the ledger line. For a free-standing overhead, you'll need to erect a post slightly taller than the desired height, mark the height on that post, and work from it as you would from a ledger.

Setting a Post

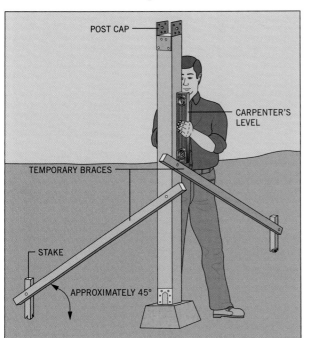

- POST CAP
- CARPENTER'S LEVEL
- TEMPORARY BRACES
- STAKE
- APPROXIMATELY 45°

Establishing a Level Line

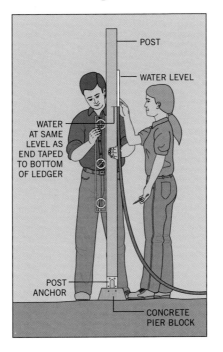

- POST
- WATER LEVEL
- WATER AT SAME LEVEL AS END TAPED TO BOTTOM OF LEDGER
- POST ANCHOR
- CONCRETE PIER BLOCK

MEASURING & MARKING POSTS Cut posts 6 to 12 inches longer than the finish length. Starting with the first post, have a helper hold it plumb on its anchor. Check two adjacent sides for plumb with a carpenter's level.

Use a line level or a water level to mark the post at the proper height for the bottom of the rafters. This will usually be level with the bottom of the ledger, but if you're using a ledger that is wider than the rafters, you'll need to measure down from the ledger's top to determine where the bottom of the rafters will fall.

Establishing a Cutting Line

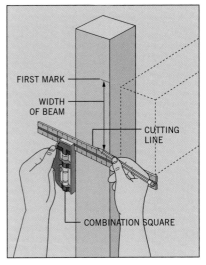

- FIRST MARK
- WIDTH OF BEAM
- CUTTING LINE
- COMBINATION SQUARE

From that mark, subtract the actual thickness (or, in this case, the "height") of any beam that will sit between the post and rafters. Also subtract any necessary drop for roof pitch and, for a sloped rafter, the small notch in the rafter's underside where it rests on the beam (see page 129). Make a new mark and, using a combination square, continue it around the post's perimeter. This is your cutting line. Repeat for the remaining posts.

CUTTING POSTS Use a circular saw or handsaw to cut the posts to length. Before permanently erecting them, seal the cut ends with a preservative and consider finishing the posts (see page 123). If your design calls for metal post-and-beam connectors, attach them to the posts before raising them.

RAISING POSTS Posts can be quite heavy so you'll probably need a helper when it comes time to position them. Before moving the first post into position, drive stakes into the ground and nail a brace made from a 1 by 2 or 1 by 3 to each stake (use only one nail so

Lifting a Beam

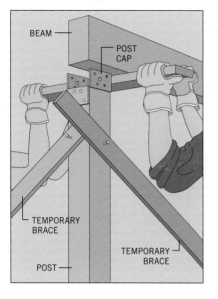

Joining Beams Over Posts

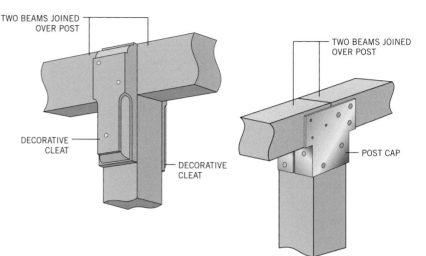

the brace can pivot). Position the stakes far enough away from the end of the post so the braces can reach midway up the post when at a 45-degree angle, as shown on page 125.

Seat the post squarely in the anchor and check for plumb using a carpenter's level on adjacent sides. Nail the braces to the post and continue to check for plumb. Then nail or lag-screw the post to its base. Finally, drive additional nails into each brace to secure the posts until the beams are seated.

SEATING BEAMS Hoisting a large beam atop a post over your head demands considerable strength; always get help for this stage of construction.

After cutting a beam to the proper length, drag it into position next to the posts and slip a short length of 2 by 4 under one end. With a helper, raise that end of the beam and maneuver it into the post cap. Partially drive in one nail to secure the beam before you lift the other end. Raise the other end using the same technique. Then finish fastening the beam to the posts.

Metal post-and-beam connectors are the strongest way to join a beam to the top of a post. Alternatively, you can nail a pair of wooden cleats to each post's top, as shown above.

BRACING POSTS & BEAMS Unless they have a steel or engineered structure, post-and-beam assemblies, particularly for free-standing patio roofs, normally require bracing for lateral stability. Roofs

less than 12 feet high usually require bracing only on the outside posts of the side not connected to the house. As shown in the illustrations below, you can make braces to be simple or highly decorative.

Mark individual braces in position and cut them on the ground. Nail them in place temporarily. Then drill pilot holes for lag screws or bolts and permanently fasten them.

Brace Styles

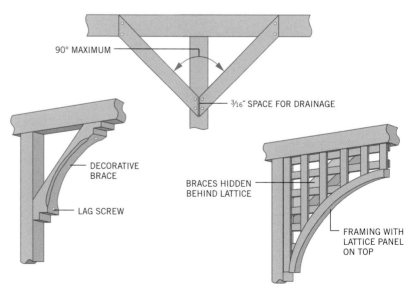

INSTALLING RAFTERS

Most patio roof and gazebo designs have roof rafters; they may be level or sloping, depending on whether the roof must shed water. Rafters spread roofing loads across beams, making it possible to use thin roofing materials that otherwise couldn't span the distances between beams. Rafters must support their own weight over open space without sagging or twisting and also support the weight of the roof covering.

RAFTER CONSTRUCTION

Methods used for building with rafters depend upon the roof's design.

ATTACHING RAFTERS TO A LEDGER

With an attached overhead, rafters are fastened to the house at one end, as discussed on page 117. Metal framing connectors make the best connections. Joist hangers can hang rafters from a ledger, but notch the rafters or use special rafter hangers for sloping rafters. If rafters will sit on top of a ledger, attach them with seismic anchors as you would attach rafters to a beam.

ATTACHING RAFTERS TO BEAMS

There are also various ways of attaching rafters to a beam. If the rafters will slope, use seismic anchors (also known as rafter ties), as shown at right. Although one standard anchor is adequate in most cases, a second one may be required diagonally across from the first one in high-wind or seismic areas; consult your building department for standards in your area. With conventional anchors, you must notch the rafters to fit or use a double-sided anchor to avoid notching.

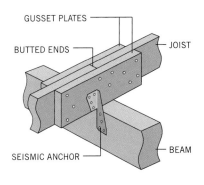

Gusset Plates Splice

GUSSET PLATES

BUTTED ENDS

JOIST

SEISMIC ANCHOR

BEAM

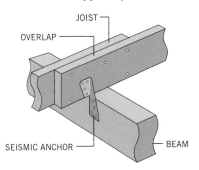

Overlapped Splice

JOIST

OVERLAP

SEISMIC ANCHOR

BEAM

ATTACHING RAFTERS TO GAZEBO HUBS

Most gazebos have a center point where roof rafters meet. To join the rafter ends, which are often cut at compound angles, a hub is used. Typical hubs are shown at left.

SPLICING RAFTERS

Where appearance allows, rafters can be spliced together end-to-end with board lumber "gusset plates." To do this, butt the ends of the rafters together over a supporting beam. Then nail two pieces of 1-by or 2-by lumber of the same width as the rafters and about 18 inches long on both sides of the splice. Or, join the members using manufactured metal splice plates.

Be sure each rafter end bears a full inch of the supporting beam. If you must splice several rafters, stagger the

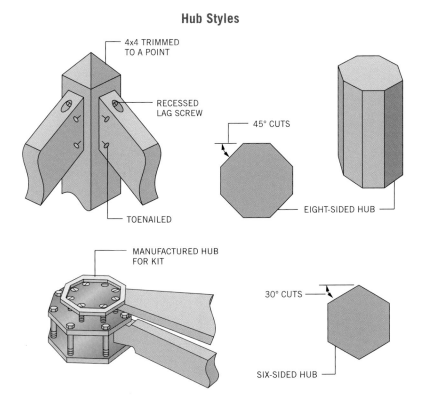

Hub Styles

4x4 TRIMMED TO A POINT

RECESSED LAG SCREW

TOENAILED

45° CUTS

EIGHT-SIDED HUB

MANUFACTURED HUB FOR KIT

30° CUTS

SIX-SIDED HUB

splices over different beams to avoid a weak substructure.

Another splicing method for rafters—though it does not utilize uniform spacing—is to overlap rafter ends supported by beams. If more than one splice is needed on a full rafter length, alternate overlapped sides.

For standard 2-inch lumber, nail both faces of each splice with six 8d or 10d common galvanized nails. This type of splicing, as shown on page 127, adds lateral stability to the rafters and may eliminate the need for bracing.

DETAILING & FASTENING RAFTERS

The time to add decorative detailing to rafters is before you lift and fasten them into place. Following are the methods for detailing, fastening, and bracing rafters.

DECORATIVE RAFTER TAILS Decoratively cutting rafter ends, as shown at right, can give a patio roof a distinctive style. You'll see many examples of decorative rafter-end treatments throughout this book. Use a saber saw for making curved cuts.

Fitting sloped rafters in place can be tricky for a novice. It's usually easiest to cut one rafter to fit and then use it as a template for the rest, but this only works if the supporting beam and ledger (or second beam) are perfectly parallel. The following procedure, illustrated on page 129, shows how to cut sloping rafters for a house-attached patio roof.

Decorative Rafter Tails

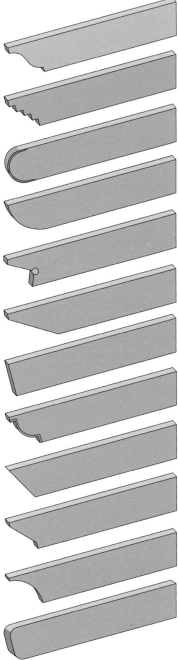

Staggered Blocking Over a Beam

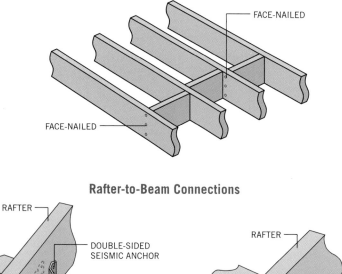

FACE-NAILED

FACE-NAILED

Rafter-to-Beam Connections

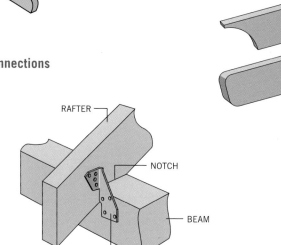

RAFTER

DOUBLE-SIDED SEISMIC ANCHOR

BEAM

RAFTER

NOTCH

BEAM

STANDARD SEISMIC ANCHOR

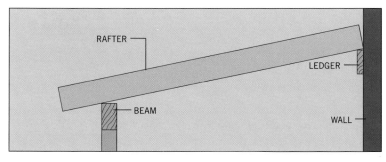

1 Lay a rafter so it rests on edge on both the beam and the ledger, making sure its lower edge makes full contact with both surfaces.

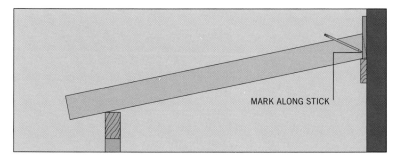

MARK ALONG STICK

2 Force the tip of the rafter snugly against the house wall; then, using a straight stick or ruler as a spacer, mark the end for making a cut that is parallel with the wall.

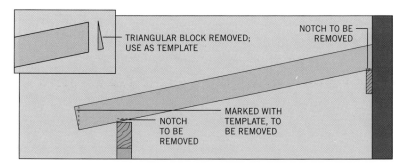

TRIANGULAR BLOCK REMOVED; USE AS TEMPLATE

NOTCH TO BE REMOVED

MARKED WITH TEMPLATE, TO BE REMOVED

NOTCH TO BE REMOVED

3 Cut the triangular piece off the rafter end where it rests on the ledger. Then use this piece as a template to trim the other end of the rafter. Finally, notch the rafter so it will seat on the beam and ledger.

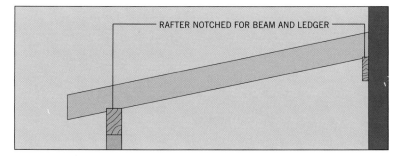

RAFTER NOTCHED FOR BEAM AND LEDGER

4 Position the rafter to check for fit; also check the fit in several other locations along the beam's length. If it fits all the way along, you will be able to use it as a template; otherwise, you'll have to repeat steps 1 to 4 with each rafter.

FASTENING TO A BEAM Where rafters rest on a beam, there are a couple of ways to fasten them, as shown opposite. You can use a double-sided seismic anchor or, if the rafter is notched, a conventional seismic anchor.

BRACING RAFTERS Where rafters span long distances or are spaced wide apart, they are prone to twist or buckle unless they're crossbraced with blocking. The width of the rafters is also a consideration; those made from 2 by 8s or larger lumber require more blocking than those made from 2 by 6s. Blocking spacing is typically determined by local codes. If rafter spans are less than 8 feet, headers nailed across the rafter ends are adequate for rafters that sit on top of beams.

Snap a chalk line across the rafters at the relevant points, then work your way across the joists, measuring and notating the lengths of blocking you'll need to cut from the rafter material. Cut and code all the blocks to correspond to their locations.

The easiest method of placing the blocks is to stagger them from one side of the chalk line to the other. By using this technique, you'll be able to face-nail the blocks; use 16d nails.

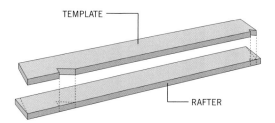

TEMPLATE

RAFTER

5 To use the rafter as a template, just lay the cut one on each of the others, mark, and cut. Check each for fit, finish all of them (see page 123), then fasten them in place.

ROOFING THE STRUCTURE

Installing roofing such as lath, lattice panels, and other open-style materials is a relatively easy—though repetitive—job. Roof coverings meant to shed rain can be more of a challenge. Still others—glass (and some plastics), steel, tar-and-gravel, and tile—are best left to professionals.

In this section you'll find information on creating open-style roofing as well as how to roof with asphalt shingles, wood shingles, and a few solid-roof variations such as siding, plywood, and corrugated panels. Characteristics of various roofing materials are discussed beginning on page 134.

The illustrations below and opposite show several types of patio roofs and two methods of building a gazebo roof—one with asphalt shingles, the other with wood shingles. The gazebo roof construction can just as easily be used on a patio roof.

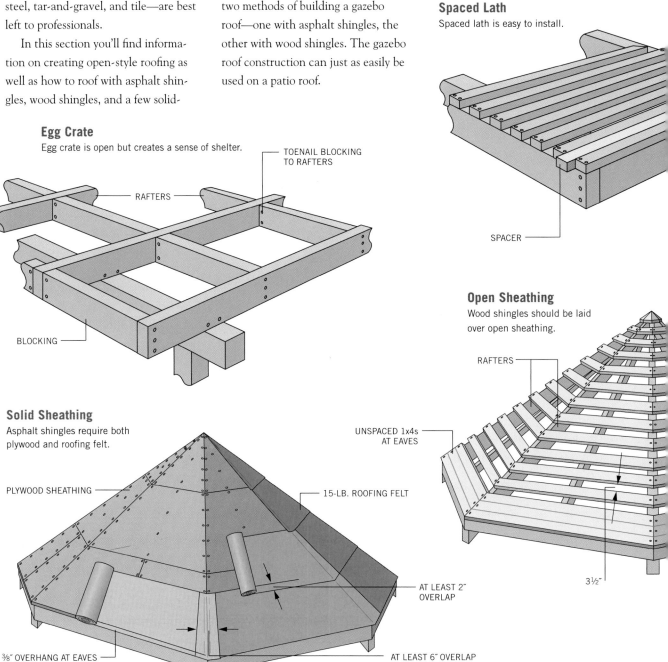

Egg Crate
Egg crate is open but creates a sense of shelter.

TOENAIL BLOCKING TO RAFTERS

RAFTERS

BLOCKING

Solid Sheathing
Asphalt shingles require both plywood and roofing felt.

PLYWOOD SHEATHING

⅜" OVERHANG AT EAVES

15-LB. ROOFING FELT

AT LEAST 2" OVERLAP

AT LEAST 6" OVERLAP AT CORNERS

Spaced Lath
Spaced lath is easy to install.

SPACER

Open Sheathing
Wood shingles should be laid over open sheathing.

RAFTERS

UNSPACED 1x4s AT EAVES

3½"

Corrugated Plastic

Corrugated plastic panels shed water but allow light.

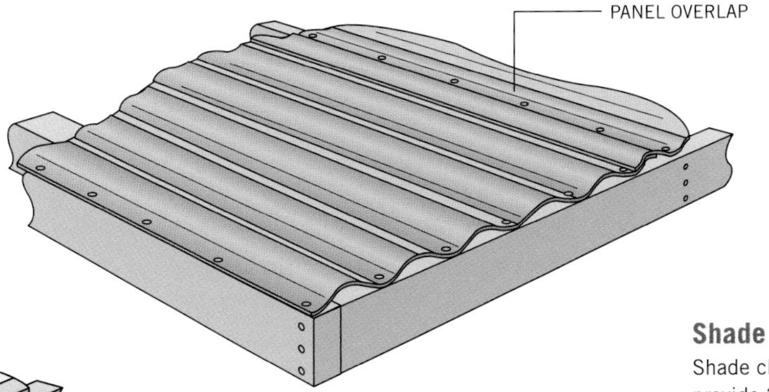

PANEL OVERLAP

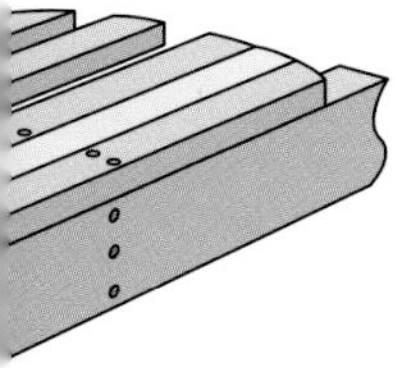

Shade Cloth

Shade cloth, depending on the weave, can provide 20 percent to 90 percent shade.

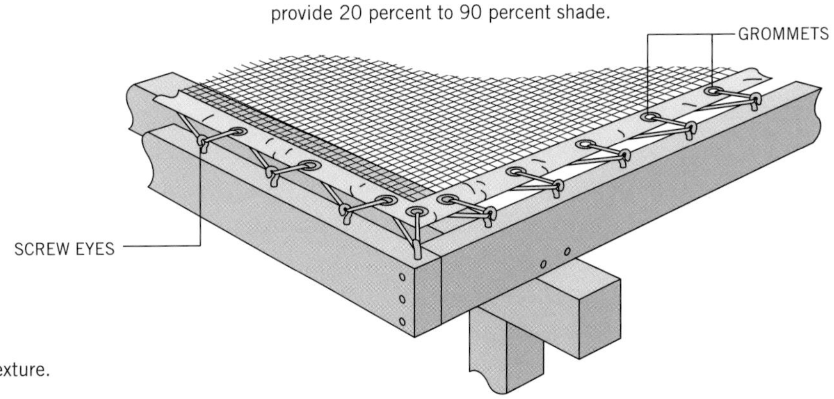

GROMMETS

SCREW EYES

Woven Reed

Woven reed offers an interesting texture.

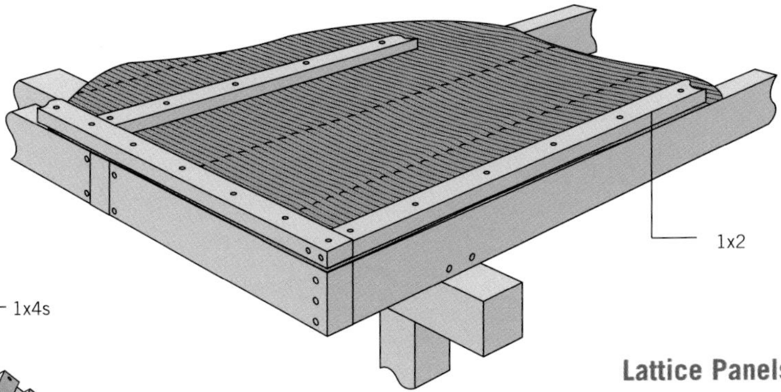

1x2

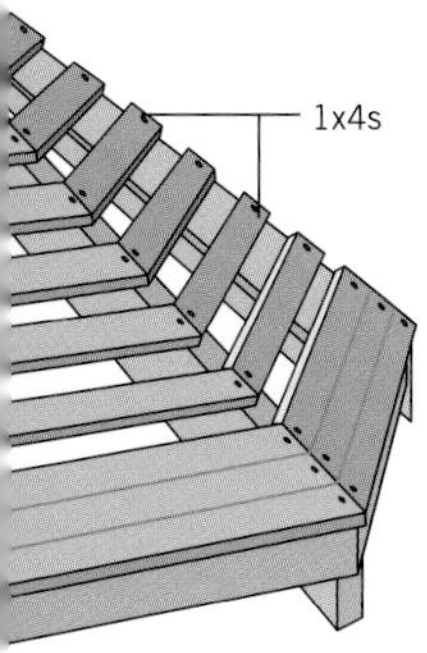

1x4s

Lattice Panels

Lattice panels can be purchased premade or you can construct them.

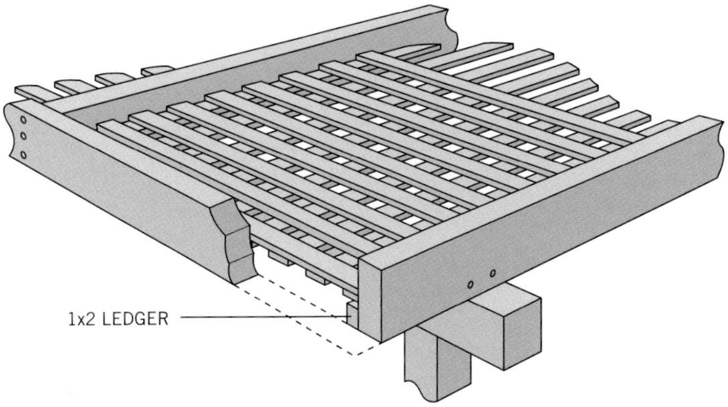

1x2 LEDGER

OPEN-STYLE ROOFING

Though the materials used for open-style roofing can range from thin lattice-work to bulky beams, the installation techniques for the various types are similar. Some can even be built apart from the structure, then installed.

ROOFING WITH LATH, BATTENS & BOARDS

Whether you're using lath, battens, boards, or larger lumber, the width of the pieces and the spacing between them will determine the effect created by your overhead.

CREATING SHADE Wood thickness and spacing can vary enormously—as can the amount of shade the variations create. For example, ⅜-inch lath laid flat and spaced 3 inches apart won't cast much shadow. But 2 by 2s spaced half an inch apart—or 1 by 3s on edge—will cast considerable shade.

Here are some spacing guidelines used by landscape architects: Space lath up to ½ inch thick from ⅜ to ¾ inch apart. For stock from ½ to 1⅛ inches thick, use a spacing of between ¾ and 1 inch. You can space 2 by 2s up to 2 inches apart under certain circumstances, but spacing them 1 to 1½ inches will make the patio more comfortable in most cases.

The right direction to run the roofing material depends on the time of day you want maximum shade. If you want the greatest relief from sun at noon, plan to run the material east-west; if you want more shade in the early morning and late afternoon, run it north-south.

It's a good idea to test your roofing material by temporarily nailing it at various spacing intervals to the rafters so you can study the effects of each configuration at different times of the day. Keep in mind too that the angle of the sun changes from season to season, not just during the course of a day.

Roof height will also affect the degree of light that falls on your patio or deck. The higher the patio roof, the more diffused the light becomes. The lower the roof, the sharper the shadows on the ground.

SUITABLE SPANS To avoid sagging and warping, be conservative about how far you span the roofing material. Don't span common lath and batten more than 2 feet. You can span 1-bys up to 3 feet, but 2 feet is better; with 1-by-2-inch stock laid on edge—or with 2 by 2s—you can span 4 feet without objectionable sagging, but the boards may warp or curve a bit. Don't span any material more than 4 feet.

Sight down lumber to check for any crown (a curve along the edge); if the material does have a crown, make sure to face it upward.

NAILING Though a little bit of twisting or bending is acceptable, boards should be evenly spaced and in perfect alignment before you nail them.

Always use corrosion-resistant nails to secure the wood to the framework. With ⅜- or ½-inch-thick lath, use 3d or 4d common or box nails. For 1-inch stock, choose 8d nails. Use 12d or 16d nails for thicker materials. Nail twice at each rafter and join cut ends directly over the rafters. If your nails split the wood, predrill the nail holes.

PREASSEMBLY To reduce your time on the rooftop, preassemble panels and fasten them as shown at left. You can make the panels practically any size, but 3 by 6 feet is close to the optimum for lightweight material. Just be sure the structural framing is true enough to receive the panels without a struggle.

Preassembled Lattice Panel

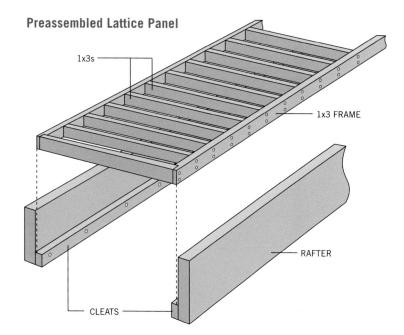

1x3s

1x3 FRAME

RAFTER

CLEATS

Fixed-louver Supports

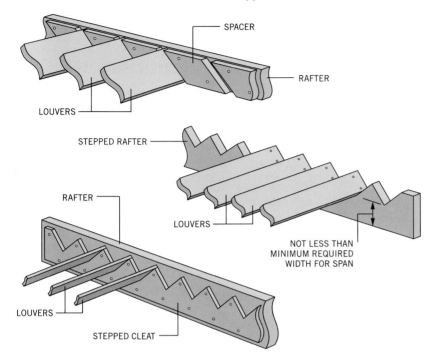

SPACER

RAFTER

LOUVERS

STEPPED RAFTER

RAFTER

LOUVERS

NOT LESS THAN
MINIMUM REQUIRED
WIDTH FOR SPAN

LOUVERS

STEPPED CLEAT

LOUVERED SLAT ROOFING

Angled louvers made from battens or boards offer an extra element of sun control. Adjustable types can give you almost any degree of light or shade throughout the day; fixed louvers can block the sun during any part of a day when it's unwanted.

LOUVER ORIENTATION Generally speaking, if you run louvers east-west, slanting the boards away from the sun, you'll block the midday sun and admit morning and afternoon sun. If you run them north-south, you'll admit either morning or afternoon sun, depending on the louvers' slant.

Since the louvered overhead is designed to block direct light for only part of the day, you'll want to figure out what time the sun is highest in the sky during summer. (See page 8 for information on seasonal sun angles.)

When figuring louvers for a pitched roof, don't forget to factor in the angle of the pitch to the angle of the sun.

INSTALLING FIXED LOUVERS Fixed louvers can be nailed directly to rafters

or they can be built in modular sections, then fastened in place. The illustrations at left show three different ways of fastening louvers to their supports. If you cut stepped rafters, be sure the width at the shallowest point is not less than that specified for the span.

For the louvers, 1 by 3s, 1 by 4s, or 1 by 6s not more than 3 feet long are usually best (the narrower the pieces, the closer they must be spaced).

INSTALLING ADJUSTABLE LOUVERS Though adjustable louvers can be exacting to build, they offer excellent sun control. If you don't want to attempt the precision work involved in making adjustable louvers, consider buying a ready-made system.

Shown below is one design for building your own system. Build the modules separately, then fasten them between the rafters. Louvers should not exceed 4 feet in length; cut them slightly shorter than the space between the rafters. You can use aluminum nails with the heads clipped off for the pins.

Home-built Adjustable Louvers

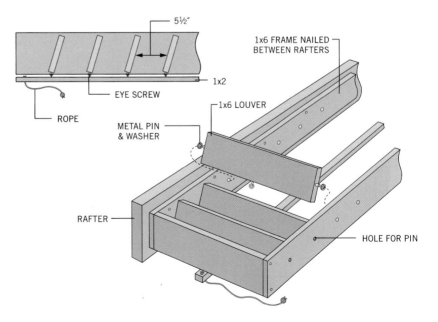

5½"

1x6 FRAME NAILED BETWEEN RAFTERS

EYE SCREW

1x2

1x6 LOUVER

ROPE

METAL PIN & WASHER

RAFTER

HOLE FOR PIN

SOLID ROOFING

Do-it-yourselfers can install any of several solid roofing materials on a patio roof or gazebo, including asphalt shingles, wood shingles, certain siding materials, and plastic or aluminum panels. Before choosing a material, consider the pitch of your new structure's roof. In addition, you may have to apply underlayment and sheathing before you can install the roofing material.

ROOF PITCH

The steeper a roof's pitch, the more likely water will roll off without penetrating. "Pitch" refers to the vertical rise measured against a standard horizontal distance of 12 inches (see the illustration at right). The term "4 in 12," applied to a roof, tells you that the roof rises vertically 4 inches for every 12 horizontal inches.

Asphalt shingles and wood shingles and shakes are designed for roofs with a 4-in-12 or greater slope. With additional underlayment, asphalt shingles can be applied to 2-in-12 slopes and wood shingles and shakes to 3-in-12 slopes. Do-it-yourself plastic and aluminum panels work well on slopes as gradual as 2 in 12—but don't expect them to hold out all water or to bear the weight of snow.

BUILDING THE ROOF'S BASE

On house roofs, asphalt shingles are normally applied over plywood sheathing with an underlayment of 15-pound roofing felt. Wood shingles are typically

Measuring Roof Pitch

Mark a line 12 inches from one end on a level and rest that end on the roof. Raise or lower the opposite end until the tool is level. Then measure the distance between the roof and the 12-inch mark to determine the pitch. If it's 3 inches, for example, the roof's pitch is "3 in 12."

Asphalt-shingle Roof Construction

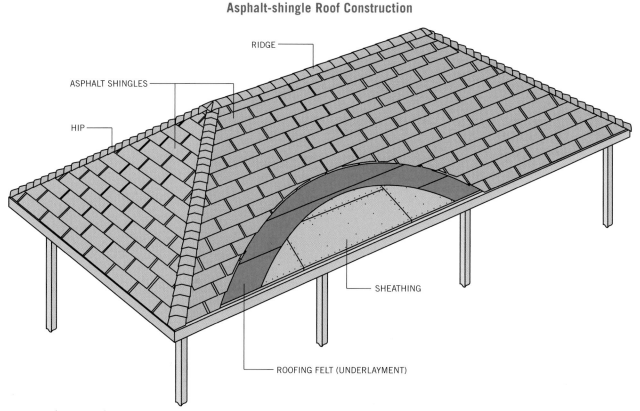

Installing Drip Edges

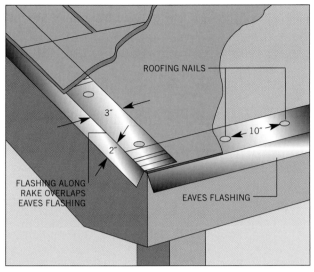

At eaves, nail a preformed metal drip edge in place before applying the roofing felt. After the felt is down, nail the drip edge along the rakes.

Installing Underlayment

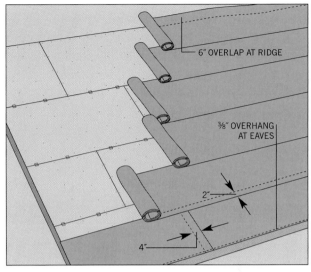

Roofing felt, a heavy, asphalt-impregnated black paper, provides an extra layer of weather protection over plywood sheathing.

laid atop spaced 1-by-4 boards. Both constructions are illustrated by the gazebo roofs shown on pages 130–131.

Patio roofs and gazebos differ from most house roofs in that they don't have ceilings to hide the construction. For that reason, solid sheathing is typically preferred. In fact, you may want to choose a higher-grade material with a good side that can be faced downward, then painted or stained.

SOLID PLYWOOD SHEATHING Though some codes permit using plywood as thin as $3/8$ inch on roofs, you'll probably want either $1/2$- or $5/8$-inch sheathing for a sturdier nailing base.

Stagger the sheathing horizontally across the rafters, centering the panel ends on rafters (leave $1/8$ inch between edges and $1/16$ inch between ends of adjoining panels to allow for expansion). Use 6d galvanized common or box nails for plywood up to $1/2$ inch thick, 8d nails for plywood $5/8$ inch and thicker. Space nails every 6 inches along the ends of each panel and every 12 inches at intermediate supports.

FLASHING Flashing protects your roof at its most vulnerable points—where the roof connects to the structure, along eaves, in valleys, or anywhere water might seep into the sheathing. Flashing is most commonly made from malleable, 28-gauge galvanized sheet metal. Plastic and aluminum flashing are available, too.

You can buy preformed flashing for drip edges and valleys or make your own. Use roofing nails to fasten it in place, positioning them where roofing or adjoining flashing will cover them. Caulk any exposed nail heads.

UNDERLAYMENT If you're using asphalt shingles, you'll need to cover the decking with roofing felt. To evenly align rows of underlayment, measure the roof carefully and snap horizontal chalk lines before you begin. Snap the first line $33 5/8$ inches above the eaves (this

allows for a $3/8$-inch overhang). Then, providing for a 2-inch overlap between strips of felt, snap each succeeding chalk line at 34 inches.

When applying felt, start at the eaves and roll the strips out horizontally along the roof, working toward the ridge or top edge. The felt should be trimmed flush at the gable overhang and overlap 6 inches at any ridges, hips, or valleys. Wherever two strips meet in a vertical line, overlap them by 4 inches.

Drive just enough roofing nails or staples to hold the felt in place until the roofing material is applied.

INSTALLING SPACED SHEATHING For wood shingles, install spaced sheathing. Lay well-seasoned 1-by-4 boards horizontally along the roof, using another 1 by 4 as a spacing guide. Fasten each board to the rafters with two 8d nails, allowing $1/8$ inch spacing where boards meet. Start your installation with solid rows of 1 by 4s at the eaves and rakes.

APPLYING ASPHALT SHINGLES

Standard three-tab asphalt shingles are the easiest roofing material to install. They are a manageable weight and a breeze to cut and nail. In addition, the 12-by-36-inch shingles, given a standard weather exposure of 5 inches, cover large areas very quickly.

Asphalt shingles are applied over a solid deck of plywood sheathing with an underlayment of 15-pound roofing felt.

CUTTING & NAILING Cut asphalt shingles facedown on a flat surface with a sharp utility knife. Hold a carpenter's square or straightedge on the cut line and score the back of the shingle with the knife. Then bend the shingle to break it on the scored line.

Choose nails that won't poke through the underside of the sheathing, typically 12-gauge, 1¼-inch-long galvanized roofing nails with ⅜-inch-diameter heads. When nailing, drive the heads snug with the surface, but be careful not to break the shingle.

LAYING SHINGLES A narrow starter row of shingles runs the length of the eaves to form a base for the first full course of shingles. When laying the successive courses of shingles, the main consideration is proper alignment—both horizontally and vertically. To horizontally align shingles that will be nailed over roofing felt, snap chalk lines.

When working with standard three-tab shingles, you can produce centered, diagonal, or random roof patterns by adjusting the length of the shingle that begins each course. Centered alignment creates the most uniform appearance but is also the most difficult pattern to achieve. Diagonal alignment is a little more forgiving since the joints of four courses in a row are offset. Random alignment produces a more rustic appearance and is the easiest of the three patterns to lay. Just offset the joints of three courses in a row by at least 3 inches.

If your project includes hip and ridge shingles, buy them ready-made or cut and bend 12-inch squares from standard shingles. Snap chalk lines along each side of the ridge and along each hip, 6 inches from the center.

Installing Asphalt Shingles

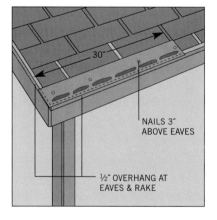

1 Lay a narrow starter course of shingles—here, 9 inches wide—along the eaves to form a base for the first full course. Trim 6 inches off the length of the first starter shingle to offset the cutouts in the starter course with the cutouts in the first full course. Use four nails for each shingle.

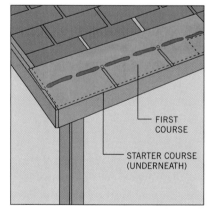

2 Lay full-width shingles for the first course, allowing a ½-inch overhang at the rakes and eaves and ¹⁄₁₆ inch between shingles. As with the starter course, use four nails per shingle.

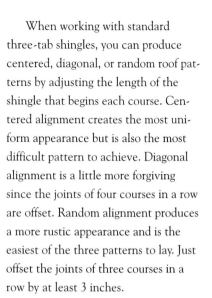

3 Snap a chalk line every 10 inches from the bottom of the first course up to the ridge. Before you start the second row of shingles, also snap vertical chalk lines from the roof ridge to one end of every shingle along the first course, or every 36 inches.

APPLYING WOOD SHINGLES

Wood shingles are installed, tapered ends uproof, on open sheathing, as shown below. If the wood has a sawn side and a rough side, install the pieces with the rough side exposed. Correct exposure for wood shingles depends on their length and the slope of the roof. Recommended exposures are shown in the chart below.

NAILING Use two rustproof nails per shingle. Choose 14½-gauge nails with 7/32-inch-wide heads, 1¼ inches in length. Place a nail ¾ inch in from each side of a shingle, 1 inch above the butt line for the next course.

TRIMMING To make straight cuts along the grain of shingles, simply slice through them with a roofer's hatchet. When it's necessary to cut a shingle across the grain, use a utility knife to score it. If the wood is thin, break it against a hard edge. Otherwise, saw it.

STARTER COURSE & FIRST COURSE Combine the starter and first courses by laying the shingles one on top of the other, as shown at right. Note that shorter shingles are used for the starter course. Overhang this double course 1½ inches at eaves and rakes. Offset joints between layers at least 1½ inches. Allow ¼ inch between shingles for the wood to expand and contract.

SUCCESSIVE COURSES When you lay the next courses, align the shingles both vertically and horizontally for proper exposure and coverage. You don't need to snap chalk lines for vertical alignment. Simply lay the random-width shingles according to this principle: Offset joints at least 1½ inches so that no joints in any three successive courses are in alignment.

Installing Hip & Ridge Shingles

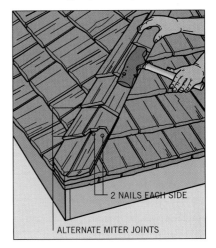

2 NAILS EACH SIDE

ALTERNATE MITER JOINTS

Installing Surface Shingles

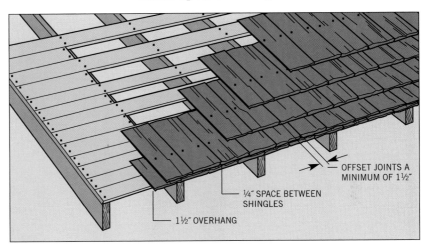

OFFSET JOINTS A MINIMUM OF 1½"

¼" SPACE BETWEEN SHINGLES

1½" OVERHANG

To align the shingles horizontally, snap a chalk line at the proper exposure over the doubled starter/first course or use your roofer's hatchet as an exposure guide. Then lay the lower edge of the next course on the chalk line and nail. Repeat, working your way up the roof until you reach the ridge or top.

At the ridge, let the last courses of shingles hang over, then snap a chalk line above the center of the ridge board and trim all the ends at once. Cover the ridge with a strip of 30-pound roofing felt at least 8 inches wide.

APPLYING HIP & RIDGE SHINGLES Using factory-made ridge and hip shingles, double the starter courses at the bottom of each hip and at the end of the ridge, as shown at top. Exposure should equal the weather exposure of the wood shingles on the roof planes. Start the ridge shingles at the end of the ridge opposite the direction of prevailing winds. Use nails long enough (usually 2 to 2½ inches) to extend into the ridge board adequately.

MAXIMUM EXPOSURE FOR WOOD SHINGLES

Size	3-in-12 to 4-in-12 slopes	Steeper slopes
16″	3¾″	5″
18″	4¼″	5½″
24″	5¾″	7½″

Note: Exposures are for No. 1 (Blue Label) quality.

ROOFING WITH SIDING

In addition to conventional asphalt and wood shingles, various other siding and panel products can provide cover for some patio roofs and gazebos. As a rule, these are not meant for heavy weather exposure—shedding rain or snow—so expect leaks and a tendency to show wear over time.

BOARD SIDING

Though it may not keep out wind-driven rain, bevel or Dolly Varden board siding may serve as a roofing material that looks good both on top and underneath. Simply cut and nail horizontal boards directly onto the rafters. For a more watertight application, mount siding boards onto roof sheathing covered with underlayment (see page 135). A typical application is shown below. Be sure the roof has a pitch of at least 4 in 12 (see page 134) since any lower pitch may allow water to penetrate.

NAILING To apply solid-board siding, use rustproof nails that are long enough to penetrate the rafters by at least 1 inch. Spiral or ring-shank nails offer better holding power than nails with smooth shanks. If the boards tend to split when nailed, predrill holes for the nails or slightly blunt the tips before nailing.

APPLYING THE FIRST BOARD First, nail a starter strip along the roof's edge. This will push the first board out to match the angle of the other boards. Position the first board so it overhangs the starter strip by ¾ inch. Then nail it in place 1 inch from the lower edge.

NAILING SUCCESSIVE BOARDS To lay out the rest of the boards, make a "story pole" from a 1 by 3 that's as long as the roof is deep. Mark the pole at intervals that equal the width of the siding boards, then transfer the marks to the edges of the roof. Apply the siding boards from bottom to top. Overlap each board 1 inch (or as required by the rabbeted edge) and nail every 6 inches, placing nails 1 inch from the lower edge.

Where boards will be end-joined, brush water repellent, stain, or primer on the ends before installation; be sure to make the joint square and snug. Slip a shingle wedge under the joint and nail each board end to it, using two nails spaced 4 inches apart; caulk the seams. Though sidings don't have special pieces for hips and ridges, you can use cedar hip and ridge shingles (see page 137). Flash as you would a shingle roof (see page 135).

INSTALLING PLYWOOD SIDING

Though roofing felt and plywood can be applied directly over rafters, this type of installation won't be very attractive from below unless the structure has a ceiling to hide the felt. The easiest way to build a ceiling is to nail ⅜-inch plywood sheets to the undersides of the rafters.

Choose a siding pattern that will allow water to run off without interruption and that has vertical shiplap edges.

Mount sheets vertically and install sheet metal Z-flashing along any horizontal joints. Allow a 1/16-inch expansion gap between sheets and caulk all seams. Before installing the plywood, brush the edges with water repellent.

NAILING Nail the sheets with rustproof common or box nails long enough to

Board Siding as Roofing

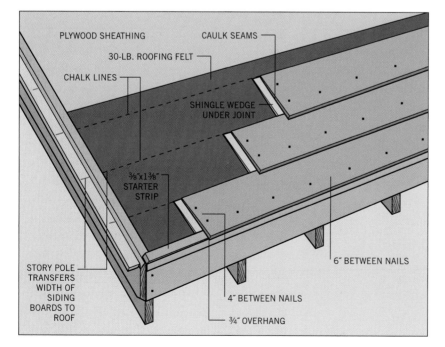

PLYWOOD SHEATHING

30-LB. ROOFING FELT

CHALK LINES

CAULK SEAMS

SHINGLE WEDGE UNDER JOINT

⅜"x1⅜" STARTER STRIP

STORY POLE TRANSFERS WIDTH OF SIDING BOARDS TO ROOF

4" BETWEEN NAILS

¾" OVERHANG

6" BETWEEN NAILS

Plywood Roofing

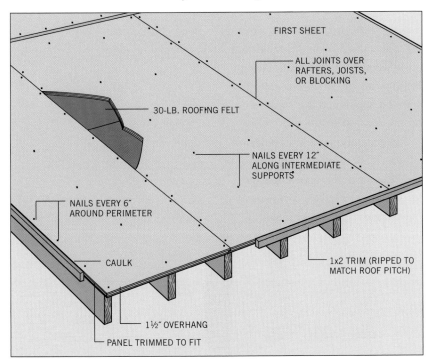

- FIRST SHEET
- ALL JOINTS OVER RAFTERS, JOISTS, OR BLOCKING
- 30-LB. ROOFING FELT
- NAILS EVERY 12" ALONG INTERMEDIATE SUPPORTS
- NAILS EVERY 6" AROUND PERIMETER
- CAULK
- 1x2 TRIM (RIPPED TO MATCH ROOF PITCH)
- 1½" OVERHANG
- PANEL TRIMMED TO FIT

Horizontal Joint

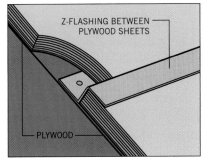

- Z-FLASHING BETWEEN PLYWOOD SHEETS
- PLYWOOD

Vertical Joint

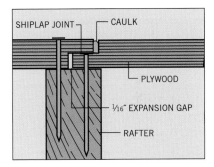

- SHIPLAP JOINT
- CAULK
- PLYWOOD
- 1⁄16" EXPANSION GAP
- RAFTER

penetrate the rafters 1½ inches. Nail every 6 inches around the perimeter of each sheet (at the rafters) and every 12 inches along intermediate supports, as shown above.

APPLYING THE FIRST SHEET Position the first sheet at an outside corner, letting its lower edge overhang the rafter tails by 1½ inches along the eaves. Center the inside edge over a rafter, orienting the shiplap edge with the upper board's edge and overlapping the lower board's edge. Then mark and use a circular saw or handsaw to trim the outer edge so it will overhang the rake about 1½ inches. Nail the sheet in place.

INSTALLING SUCCESSIVE SHEETS Butt the next sheet against the first, interlocking the shiplap edges and leaving a 1⁄16-inch expansion gap. Nail the sheet and caulk the seams. Apply remaining sheets in the same way.

INSTALLING CORRUGATED PANELS

Corrugated panels made from plastic or aluminum can provide reasonably watertight roofing on slopes as low as 2 in 12. The 26-inch-wide panels, installed with a 2-inch overlap, are designed to connect to rafters on 24-inch centers. Support the panels along the seams and install crossbracing every 5 feet to prevent sagging.

CUTTING & NAILING Cut plastic or aluminum panels with a fine-toothed handsaw or a power saw equipped with a plywood-cutting or abrasive blade. Be sure to wear protective glasses or goggles when cutting.

Predrill nail holes, backing the panel with a scrap block as you drill. Special aluminum twist nails with neoprene collars under the heads are made for securing plastic and aluminum panels. Be sure to nail through the crowns

of the corrugations as shown below. Nail every 12 inches.

To make joints watertight where they overlap, sandwich a bead of caulking compound between the lapped edges before you nail. Generally, the best caulks for this purpose are those that remain flexible, such as silicone.

Corrugated Roof

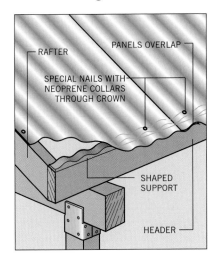

- RAFTER
- PANELS OVERLAP
- SPECIAL NAILS WITH NEOPRENE COLLARS THROUGH CROWN
- SHAPED SUPPORT
- HEADER

SCREENING OUTDOOR ROOMS

In some regions, mosquitoes and other insects can make a gazebo or patio area intolerable unless it is protected by screening.

Fortunately, adding screening to a porch or gazebo, or to a patio roof that can be easily framed-in, is a fairly straightforward task. Two methods can be used.

The easiest method is to install 1-by-1 stops on the wooden posts and framing of the structure, staple screening to them, and cover the staples and screening edges with a special molding called screen bead. The one problem with this approach is that the screens are not removable.

The second approach, shown here, requires more time and effort but results in removable screening. This involves making screened frames and mounting them in the openings.

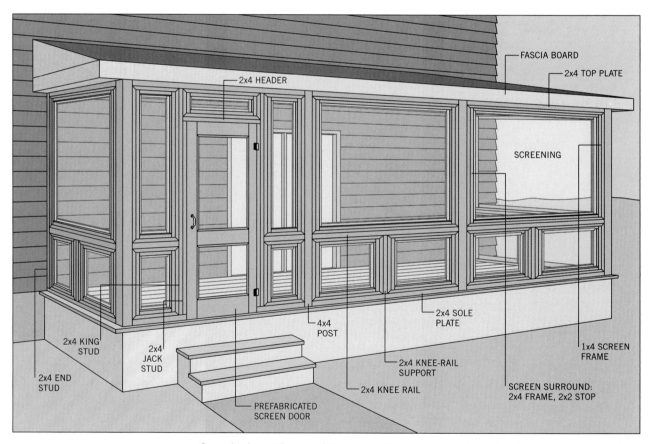

Screening in a patio or porch is not complex providing the roof fully overhangs the surface below. Openings are framed by 4-by-4 posts and 2-by-4 studs, sole plates, top plates, knee rails, and knee-rail supports. Screen surrounds consist of 2-by-4 frames and 2-by-2 stops. Screen frames fashioned from 1 by 4s are screwed to the stops for easy removal. The doorway king studs, jack studs, and header are positioned to accommodate a prefabricated screen door.

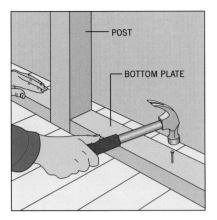

1 Attach pressure-treated 2-by-4 bottom plates between the structure's posts and 2-by-4 top plates between the post tops. Leave a doorway opening for a commercial screen door (purchase this first). For information on fasteners, see page 106.

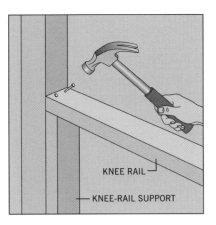

2 Cut 2-by-4 knee rails to fit between the posts, and cut 2-by-4 supports for each end of each rail. Toenail the knee-rail supports to the bottom plate and nail them to the posts. Then toenail the knee rail to the posts.

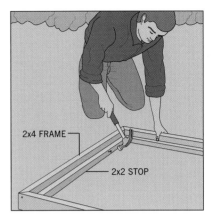

3 Assemble frames of beveled 2 by 4s to fit in the openings formed by the support members. Attach 2-by-2 stops flush with the outside edge of the frames.

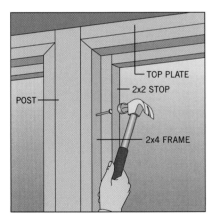

4 Nail the screen surrounds into place in the openings. Check the corners for square as you work and adjust the surrounds if necessary.

5 Measure the openings, then assemble 1 by 4s as screen frames to fit the openings. Join the frames at the corners with L-brackets. Cut screening slightly larger than each frame opening, pull it taut, and fasten it to the frames with rustproof staples every 2 inches. Trim off the excess screening.

6 Secure the screen frames to the 2-by-2 stops with galvanized screws, driven at an angle. To remove the screens for repair or storage, just remove the screws.

RESOURCES

GAZEBO KITS

Amdega Machin Conservatories
(800) 922-0110
www.amdega.com

Brite Millwork
(800) 265-6021
www.britemanufacturing.com

Caldera Spas & Baths
(800) 669-1881
www.calderaspas.com

Cumberland Woodcraft
(800) 367-1884
www.cumberlandwoodcraft.com

Moultrie Mfg. Co.
(800) 841-8674
www.moultriemfgco.com

Vixen Hill Mfg. Co.
(800) 423-2766
www.vixenhill.com

COLUMNS

Chadsworth's 1-800 Columns
(800) 265-8667
www.columns.com

Fypon, Inc.
(800) 537-5349
www.fypon.com

Moultrie Mfg. Co.
(800) 841-8674
www.moultriemfgco.com

NMC Focal Point
(800) 662-5550
www.focalpointap.com

Outwater Plastic Industries, Inc.
(800) 835-4400
www.archpro.com

Vintage Wood Works
(903) 356-2158
www.vintagewoodworks.com

LATTICE

Brite Millwork (wood & vinyl)
(800) 265-6021
www.britemanufacturing.com

Permalatt Products (vinyl)
(888) 457-4342
www.permalatt.com

ASSOCIATIONS

APA–The Engineered Wood Assn.
(253) 565-6600
www.apawood.org

Asphalt Roofing Manufacturers Assn.
(202) 207-0917
www.asphaltroofing.org

California Redwood Assn.
(888) 225-7339
www.calredwood.org

Cedar Shake & Shingle Bureau
(604) 820-7700
www.cedarbureau.org

National Paint and Coatings Assn.
(202) 462-6272
www.paint.org

National Sunroom Assn.
(785) 271-0208
www.glasswebsite.com

Screen Manufacturers Assn.
(561) 533-0991
www.screenmfgassociation.org

Southern Pine Council
(504) 443-4464
www.sfpa.org

Western Red Cedar Lumber Assn.
(604) 684-0266
www.wrcla.org

Western Wood Products Assn.
(503) 224-3930
www.wwpa.org

PHOTOGRAPHY CREDITS

Scott Atkinson, 123
Ernest Braun, 16 bottom right, 20, 78
Karen Bussolini, 6 bottom left
Ken Chen, 22
Stephen Cridland, 7 bottom left
Dalton Pavilions Inc., 10 bottom right
Derek Fell, 7 top right, 17
Jay Graham, 74
Jamie Hadley, 94
Jerry Harpur, 14 middle right, 18
Philip Harvey, 10 bottom left, 12 bottom left, 26, 42, 46, 104, 109
Jean-Claude Hurni, 6 top right, 21, 66, 90
Charles Mann, 14 bottom left, 16 top left
Sylvia Martin, 54
Jack McDowell, 70, 82
Norman A. Plate, 103, 105, 106, 107, 110, 111, 112, 113
Marvin Sloben, 38
Chad Slattery, 6 lower right
Southern Progress Corporation, 11
Ron Sutherland/The Garden Picture Library, 15
Michael S. Thompson, 58
Don Vandervort, 13 top left, 108
David Wakeley, 5
Jesse Walker, 19
Deidra Walpole, 13 lower left
Peter O. Whitely, 12 bottom right
Tom Wyatt, 30, 34, 50, 62, 86, 98

DESIGN CREDITS

The Berger Partnership, 12 bottom left
M. Bollinger, 16 top left
The Brickman Group, Ltd., 17
Dalton Pavilions Inc., 10 bottom right
Jim Long, 14 bottom left
Joleen & Tony Morales, 12 bottom right
Van-Martin Rowe Design, 10 bottom left

INDEX